# *Finance*
## *ARCHITECTURE*

## Egg of Colombus [183]
### Visual Architecture's

`applied concepts that work better than*
*"5 Blind men and an Elephant's"* [59]
## Corporate Finance Experts

A Finance Construction Engineering
*from*
# Steve Asikin

An On-line edition,
*Finance ARCHITECTURE*
**Steve Asikin**
Cover:
ISBN is 1453829547 and EAN-13 is 9781453829547
By CreateSpace

Cover:;
By I-Proclaim
http://www.i-proclaim.com/project-cover-art-
preview.asp?project=FBF48F22-BEEA-48B8-80B1-
CD25561AAC78

1$^{st}$ (paperback) edition Published in Indonesia 2010
Cakrawala Buana Indonesia Publishing,
Jl. Radio Dalam Raya No.21, Gandaria Utara, Jakarta
Selatan, INDONESIA, evetsnikisa@gmail.com

# PREFACE

This essay is _significantly against_ to any others, dedicated only for all the **geniuses** and **novices** in Finance. Genius are very smart people who can make improvements to fundamental concepts that bad. On the contrary, novices come with fresh approach and willing to work honestly.

_This essay is prohibited and extremely dangerous to people who has only **average** or **medium** skills in Finance, because this will tell them only the truth, that might be different than many difficult unuseful corporate finance and finance engineering knowledges they have learned before._

At least 6 (six) things already achieved by this essay, consecutively:

**1** This is a nice, interesting and challenging treatise, written in plain English that is easy to be understood, by most of the people of our world. Readers can follow the data, ideas and aesthetical beauty involved.

**2** This is a medium of idealism and charity. Twenty percent (20%) of its profit will be donated, to support effort to simplify world complex financial engineeering works.

**3** This is a financial construction, using many nice and easy graphic models to help corporate finance healthier

**4** This is a book of quiz and puzzles. Smart reader can enjoy them and less clever one can understand better by doing those difficult real life in the beauty of architecture.

**5** This is a book of fundamental stock-echange corpotrate finance. All ideas, tips and clues are useful.

**6** This is truly a book of architectural engineering. All constructional techniques are well packaged visually.

# TABLE OF CONTENTS

# FINANCE ARCHITECTURE RESUME

Is finance architecture or financial architecture an architecture or a finance matter? It's an *ARCHITECTURE*, like the Japanese architecture, modern architecture, Islamic architecture, bridge architecture, computer architecture etc. The finance one, called *architecture finance* or architectural finance, which means financing the architectural expenses.

Why it is talked more by financial experts than the *architectural* ones? As *engineer*, architect normally doesn't knowing much about finance and better keep their mouth shut. On the other hand the financial experts knows nothing about the *architecture*, but very confident to talk numbers and arts in above them. Hopefully they never make a claim as expert in finance *law*, finance *politics*, finance *medicine*, finance *explosive*, finance *biology* and finance *theology*.

Sure, this book can be very beneficial for both the architect who want to learn finance and also for the finance expert who want to study architecture. The first one can learn this *easier*, but the second one can have greater benefit after reading the real finance architecture book. The book will tell how much the finance will get benefit if use architecture as its tool for better analysis and explanation.

*AGAINST* many other false teachings in other books with similar title, this *architectural book* will use more graphics and box diagrams to explain the financial concepts better. So then reader can comprehend it better!

The **A-Z** *financial abbreviation* used, help making mathematical computations shorter and easier. There are exactly 26 items from **A** to **Z** of *IFRS* (Intenational Financial Reporting Standard). Nothing used twice and nothing unrepresented there. *It's very nice and simple!*

The **IFRS'** (*International Finance Reporting Standard*'s) Income Statement (*I/S*) architecture will be: **(S-V)=M** while **(M-F)=O** and **(O-I)=B** then **(B-T)=A** for **(A-D)=R** and **(D-Y)=H**, which is graphically drawn as:

| S | V |   |   |   |   |   |
|---|---|---|---|---|---|---|
|   | M | F |   |   |   |   |
|   |   | O | I |   |   |   |
|   |   |   | B | T |   |   |
|   |   |   |   | A | D | Y |
|   |   |   |   |   |   | H |
|   |   |   |   | R |   |   |

While their abbreviation stands as follows:

  **S**= Sales or revenue
  **V**= Variable expenses or direct cost of goods
  **M**= Margin of contribution
  **F**= Fixed expenses
  **O**= Operational surplus
  **I**= Investments or financial expenses
  **B**= Before tax earnings
  **T**= Tax of periodic income
  **A**= After tax earnings
  **D**= Dividend paid
  **Y**= Yielding tax of dividend
  **H**= Home taken or net dividend
  **R**= Retained earnings to add utilized equity

The diagram of boxes here is the geometric short expressions of <u>all rule</u> and laws found in *Income Statement*.

The **IFRS'** (*International Finance Reporting Standard's*) Balance-sheet (**B**/**S**) architecture will be: **W=(C+N)=(E+L)**, at **N=(K+J+P)**, on **E=(U+R)** and **L=(X+Q)** at **X=(G+Z)**. which is graphically drawn as:

| K | C | W | L | X | G |
|---|---|---|---|---|---|
| J |   |   |   |   | Z |
| P |   |   |   | Q |   |
|   | N |   | E | U |   |
|   |   |   |   | R |   |

While their abbreviation stands as follows:
>**W**= Wealth or total assets
>**C**= Current assets
>**N**= Non current assets
>**K**= Kind of cash and near cash
>**J**= Job or trade account receivables
>**P**= Procurred inventory or reserve stocks
>**L**= Liabilities or total debts
>**E**= Equity or capital of the busness owner
>**U**= Utilized or equity at the beginning of period
>**R**= Retained earnings from Income Statement
>**Q**= Quoted long-term debts or long-term liabilities
>**X**= Xpress or current liabilities (less than a year)
>**G**= Goods or trade account payables
>**Z**= Zero or un-trade related current liabilities

The diagram of boxes here is the geometric short expressions of all rule and laws found in Balance-sheet (**B**/**S**) at *IFRS* system. It can be <u>applied</u> for <u>various</u> reports.

This standardized **ABCD** items can easily package accurately all major sub-*IFRS* financial statements like the British, European, US and global world systems. So then they can easily be compared and combined ass necessary.

This book works on 13 (thirteen) world finance well fame architecture *skyscraper*[17]. **1**)Boeing[21], **2**)Wal-Mart[22], **3**)Mc Donalds[23], **4**)Microsoft[24], **5**)Mitsubishi[25], **6**)Mitsui[26], **7**)Samsung[27], **8**)Hyundai[28], **9**)Daimler-Benz[29], **10**)BMW[30], **11**) British Petroleum[31], **12**)Carefour[32] and **13**)Nestle[33]. Yes, 4 US, 2 Korean, 2 German, 2 Japan, 1 UK, 1 French and 1 Swiss *famous giant* global world-wide companies.

The reader also shown their latest web address, so then some people who really want to enjoy their complex original difficulties may do cross-check with them directly.

This is just to show the evidence that visual finance architecture can enable us to learn them nicely and quickly without ever loosing sight to any single significant financial aspect involved. They are simpler, nicer and more precise.

It employ **A** to **Z** capital letter abbreviations for all financial items to be coherence with the English letters that can be esily found in many type machines world-wide. Some abbreviations may seem strange but still easily understood. We avoid duplications to make their algebraic computation be much shorter, easier and more accurate.

The **W, placed in the middle** is because it represents the total of all assets on its left and also as the total of all the liabilities on its right. Architecturally the traditional finace T-account is not efficient because two times stating the total, while keeping the base of the T-figure empty.

We confirm that I/S is periodical while the B/S is a moment opname valid only for the period the financial statement made. Its form should always follow its function!

The-26 **IFRS'** (*International Finance Reporting Standard*'s) ratios consist of 13 financial architecture <u>key-piles</u>[33] and 13 others <u>locked-stones</u>[34]. The-13 <u>key-piles</u> are:

   **c**= Current ratio= $(C/X)$
   **d**= Dividend paid portion to after tax = $(D/A)$
   **f**= Fix expenses portion to revenue= $(F/S)$
   **g**= Goods or trade account payable days= $(360G/V)$
   **i**= Investment or financial portion to revenue= $(I/S)$
   **j**= Job or trade account receivable days= $(360J/S)$
   **l**= Leverage or gearing = debt equity ratio
        = *DER*= $(L/E)$
   **p**= Procurred inventory days= $(360P/V)$
   **q**= Quick or acid test ratio= $(C\text{-}P)/X$
   **s**= Sales or revenue growth to previous= $(S/S'\text{-}1)$
   **t**= Tax rate or portion to before tax earnings= $(T/B)$
   **v**= Variable expenses portion to revenue= $(V/S)$
   **y**= Yielding tax of the dividend paid= $(Y/D)$

The 13 (thirteen) <u>locked-stone</u> dimensions are:

   **a**= After tax return on asset= $(A/W)$
   **b**= Before tax return on asset= $(B/W)$
   **e**= Equity return= return on equity= *ROE*= $(R/E)$
   **h**= Home taken dividend to utilized equity= $(H/U)$
   **k**= Kind of cash liquidity ratio= $(K/X)$
   **m**= Market-run or asset turn-over= *ATO*= $(S/W)$
   **n**= NPM= net profit margin= $(R/S)$
   **o**= Operational surplus to asset return= $(O/W)$
   **r**= Return of net earnings on assets= *ROA*= $(R/W)$
   **u**= Utilized return on starting equity = $(R/U)$
   **w**= Working capital days required= $(g\text{-}p\text{-}j)$
   **x**= Xpress or current to total debt portion= $(X/L)$
   **z**= Zero trade liability portion of total debts= $(Z/L)$

# INTRODUCTION: Beyond *Geometric Finance*[7]

Even a *common architect*, must <u>know the geometry</u> better than the <u>best world class topologic mathematician.</u> Mathematician works with its number and *abstractions*, but the architect on <u>daily basis</u> works <u>artistically on the detail</u> of things, much harder than the distorted <u>Platonic</u> forms.

Take <u>Claymath</u>[1] *millennium problem* for instance, especially the <u>Perelman's</u>[2] solution on the <u>Poincare</u>[3] conjecture (difficult mathematic, but simple form problem).

On 2002 many Indonesian (PSAI-ITB) architects knows that it is just a <u>decompressed balloon situation.</u> As long as it's a super tight elastic durable balloon, covering any shape of many goods inside. It if can be decompressed by the super anti-compressor from its center, it will perfectly, tightly and sticky cover all surfaces. What ever complex things inside it, if the balloon could always be tightened then all things <u>will be reduced</u> to its <u>center point</u>.

The same thing will appears difficult for the world-class topology mathematician, because they are working on <u>complex algebra</u> and <u>abstractions</u>. It is much easier for the architects, because they just think staying in the center of *big balloon* <u>covering roof, tree</u> and <u>chimney</u> of their house. They <u>can prove it,</u> but off course <u>not with a Calculus way</u>.

Can any accountant, finance expert and economist compete with <u>world's topologic mathematician</u> in finance architecture? We *do not* think so. Can they compete with real three or <u>many dimensional</u> topological architects? *No!*

Finance architecture need good understanding of at least <u>2-dimensional geometric</u> finance. Most architects had passed spatial intelligence test, some mathematician will, but <u>only few</u> great accountant and financial experts can.

## Finance Ratios are *Aesthetic Elements*, not *Hurdles*

Like in common architecture, the finance one must start with <u>TOR= *terms of reference*</u> and specific written objective of project management. Architecture is different than just building or measures, it is truly an <u>artistic</u> process based on scientific constraints and <u>engineering capabilities</u>.

It is normal that a common share holder expecting 30% <u>sales growth,</u> <u>cost of goods sold</u> less than 80% of its revenue, with <u>fix expenses</u> not exceeding 10% its <u>revenue</u>, investment and <u>financial charges</u> not more than 5% its revenue, paying <u>tax</u> according to normal rate of 30%, its before tax earnings, paying <u>dividends</u> 40% of its <u>after tax</u> earnings. Starting from the existing equity, controlling the corporate <u>leverage</u> at about 99%, procured <u>inventory</u> not more than 80% <u>inventory days</u> today, <u>current ratio</u> at 1.5 times current liabilities, <u>quick ratio</u> 1.10% of its current liabilities and goods or <u>trade payable days at least 150%</u> longer than exist now. Can all be <u>achieved at same time</u>?

Yes, but could you as the financial architects show them all the financial statements items <u>passing all their 13</u> requirements? How about the other <u>financial professionals</u> and <u>professor of finance</u>? Can they do that? No, they can't.

The best they can do is just *sensitifity analysis*[4]. We can also see what it made by <u>world class experts</u>[5] like <u>Evans and Damodaran</u>[6]. Let's try the *geometric finance*[7] and *finance architecture*[8]. Wonderful, this <u>totally below</u> every standard of architecture, they are totally finance guy who <u>knows very nothing</u> about the <u>architecture</u>. We do not think that any of them could <u>pass the lowest standard</u> of <u>American Insitute of Architects</u>[9]. So, what they're doing? It's <u>against standard of truth</u> and <u>violating the science</u>. Oh!

What is *IFRS*? Developed by the American Institute of Certified <u>Public Accountant</u> (***CPA***s), International Financial Reporting Standards *(IFRS)[10]* is comprehensive resources for <u>accounting professionals, auditors, financial</u> managers and other. Since the case of Enron[11], we know the danger of not truly implementing the financial safety standard. Especially for different accounting practices in many areas, all over our world (as Europe[12] and Britain[13]).

The most important subject in economy suppose to be real **accounting**, not <u>macro</u> concepts and nor <u>managerial</u> tricks and method. It has the <u>advantage of double recording</u> to make a cross check (or check and recheck) to make sure that the financial transaction recorded and used as proper.

Each transaction recorded both in the <u>material side</u> (***Dr***= debit record) and the historical sources side (***Cr***= credit record). Those records <u>handled by different persons</u> and economic unit along its transaction, but finally both of them come to the same auditor who <u>verifiy those validity</u>.

The world's 2008 economic crisis make this method stronger by adding <u>*IFRS*</u>= *International Finance Reporting Standard* to all the world accounting system. It is even better than the great system <u>*GAAP*</u>= *Generally Accepted Accounting Principles* that widely used in the world before.

After examining  their differences in stating costs, balancing the income statement, and rating their liquidity problems, we come that they must be translated to a nicer and simpler visual[14] common of  **ABCD** to **Z** format. Each capital character in represent its-26 <u>major financial items</u>.

# Easier than Noble Winners'[15], but More *Beautiful*

The ***IFRS***' (International Finance Reporting Standard's) Income Statement (***I/S***) architecture, will be: **(S-V)=M** while **(M-F)=O** and **(O-I)=B** then **(B-T)=A** for **(A-D)=R** and **(D-Y)=H**, which is graphically drawn as:

| S | V | | | | | | | | | |
|---|---|---|---|---|---|---|---|---|---|---|
| | M | F | | | | | | | | |
| | | O | I | | | | | | | |
| | | | B | T | | | | | | |
| | | | | A | D | Y | | | | |
| | | | | | | H | | | | |
| | | | | R | | | | | | |

While their abbreviation stands as follows:

    **S**= Sales or revenue
    **V**= Variable expenses or direct cost of goods
    **M**= Margin of contribution
    **F**= Fixed expenses
    **O**= Operational surplus
    **I**= Investments or financial expenses
    **B**= Before tax earnings
    **T**= Tax of periodic income
    **A**= After tax earnings
    **D**= Dividend paid
    **Y**= Yielding tax of dividend
    **H**= Home taken or net dividend
    **R**= Retained earnings to add utilized equity

The diagram of boxes here, is the geometric short expressions of all <u>rule and laws</u> found in Income Statement.

# Be Visual, Throw All Dirts of Accounting *Myths*[16]

The *IFRS*' (International Finance Reporting Standard's) Balance-sheet (*B/S*) architecture will be: **W=(C+N)=(E+L),** at **N=(K+J+P),** on **E=(U+R)** and **L=(X+Q)** at **X=(G+Z).** which is graphically drawn as:

| K | C | W | L | X | G |
|---|---|---|---|---|---|
| J |   |   |   |   | Z |
| P |   |   |   | Q |   |
|   | N |   | E | U |   |
|   |   |   |   | R |   |

While their abbreviation stands as follows:

**W**= Wealth or total assets
**C**= Current assets
**N**= Non current assets
**K**= Kind of cash and near cash
**J**= Job or trade account receivables
**P**= Procurred inventory or reserve stocks
**L**= Liabilities or total debts
**E**= Equity or capital of the busness owner
**U**= Utilized or equity at the beginning of period
**R**= Retained earnings from Income Statement
**Q**= Quoted long-term debts or long-term liabilities
**X**= Xpress or current liabilities (less than a year)
**G**= Goods or trade account payables
**Z**= Zero or un-trade related current liabilities

The diagram of boxes here is the geometric short expressions of all rule and laws found in Balance-sheet (**B/S**) at *IFRS* system. It can be applied for various reports.

# CHAPTER-I: Finance Architecture *Sky-scraper*[17]:

The **Samsung Group** (Korean: 삼성 그룹) is a multinational conglomerate incorporated, headquartered at Samsung Town, Seoul, South Korea. It's the South Korea's largest chaebol and the world's largest conglomerate by revenue with an annual gross income of US $173.4 billion in 2008. The meaning of the Korean hanja (*kanji*, or *kanshe*) word *Samsung* (三星) is "tri-star" or "three stars".[18]

| 89,773 | 68,403 | | | | | |
|---|---|---|---|---|---|---|
| latest | 21,370 | 10,405 | | | | |
| | | 10,965 | 124 | | | |
| | | | 10,841 | 1,192 | | |
| | | | | 9,649 | - | - |
| previous | | | | | | - |
| 72,953 | | | | 9,649 | | |

**Samsung-09**

| 2,142 | 12,067 | 86,024 | 19,199 | 16,550 | 4,785 |
|---|---|---|---|---|---|
| 6,291 | | | | | 11,765 |
| 3,634 | | | | 2,649 | |
| 73,957 | | | 66,825 | 57,176 | |
| | | | | 9,649 | |

Can you tell us, where are it's **A** to **Z** position?

# Accounting *Heritage*[19] and Traditional Buildings

Before the Samsung become like the end 0f 2009 figure, the older Samsung financial architecture already exist and sure, in finance architecture, we should also had its previous financial picture as they stated as past data in the same financial statements.

| 72,953 | 55,381 | | | | | |
|---|---|---|---|---|---|---|
| latest | 17,572 | 11,614 | | | | |
| | | 5,958 | 50 | | | |
| | | | 5,908 | 382 | | |
| | | | | 5,526 | - | - |
| previous | | | | | | - |
| - | | | | | 5,526 | |

**Samsung-08**

| 2,360 | 9,268 | 72,519 | 14,406 | 11,721 | 2,388 |
|---|---|---|---|---|---|
| 3,090 | | | | | 9,333 |
| 3,818 | | | | 2,684 | |
| | 63,251 | | 58,113 | 52,588 | |
| | | | | 5,526 | |

What's your opinion? Does these 2 (two) visuals of their financial statement makes any sense to you? At least it already shorter. Surprisingly these 2 (two) pictures disclose more finance info. Certainly, we will show you the proof!

# Bill of Quantity[20] for the Accounting *Mega Structure*[21]

Architectural starts with the construction budgeting, before it translated to physical design. Please remember that the architectural building we analyze consist of **A-Z** items, here is it's **A** to **M** difference both in *absolute* amount (+) and <u>finance geometry</u> *proportional growth* (%).

|   | 2009 | 2008 | (+) | (%) |
|---|------|------|-----|-----|
| A | 9,649 | 5,526 | 4,123 | 74.61% |
| B | 10,841 | 5,908 | 4,933 | 83.49% |
| C | 12,067 | 9,268 | 2,799 | 30.20% |
| D | - | - | - | #DIV/0! |
| E | 66,825 | 58,113 | 8,712 | 14.99% |
| F | 10,405 | 11,614 | (1,209) | -10.41% |
| G | 4,785 | 2,388 | 2,397 | 100.37% |
| H | - | - | - | #DIV/0! |
| I | 124 | 50 | 74 | 148.15% |
| J | 6,291 | 3,090 | 3,201 | 103.60% |
| K | 2,142 | 2,360 | (218) | -9.24% |
| L | 19,199 | 14,406 | 4,794 | 33.28% |
| M | 21,370 | 17,572 | 3,798 | 21.61% |

It is very important for the architect to assesss its existing financial structure capability, before making any improvement plan. Architect must play exactly <u>within constraints</u>. It's a <u>creative design</u>, not just a free expression.

# Specification[22] for the Corporate Finance *Blue-print*[23]

Here also its N to Z items, show the differences between 2009 and 2008 performance. Since these A to Z item had visually presented, every body could understand it well, even though they do not very good in finance.

|   | 2009 | 2008 | (+) | (%) |
|---|------|------|-----|-----|
| N | 73,957 | 63,251 | 10,706 | 16.93% |
| O | 10,965 | 5,958 | 5,007 | 84.03% |
| P | 3,634 | 3,818 | (184) | -4.81% |
| Q | 2,649 | 2,684 | (35) | -1.30% |
| R | 9,649 | 5,526 | 4,123 | 74.61% |
| S | 89,773 | 72,953 | 16,820 | 23.06% |
| T | 1,192 | 382.32 | 810 | 211.78% |
| U | 57,176 | 52,588 | 4,588 | 8.73% |
| V | 68,403 | 55,381 | 13,022 | 23.51% |
| W | 86,024 | 72,519 | 13,505 | 18.62% |
| X | 16,550 | 11,721 | 4,829 | 41.20% |
| Y | - | - | - | #DIV/0! |
| Z | 11,765 | 9,333.26 | 2,432 | 26.05% |

Excellent financial experts could get more benefit by the visual finance architecture and 2 (two) differences shown in absolute number (+) and in proportion (%). Visual finance architecture really made financial understanding better. This is shorter and more make sense.

# The *CADD[24] Visualization* on Finance Architecture

Samsung standardized **ABCD** items can easily package accurately all major sub-*IFRS* financial statements like the British, European, US and global world systems. At the end of 2009 Samsung perform best between <u>13 (thirteen) world finance </u>architecture's famous skyscraper: **1)**Boeing[25], **2)**Wal-Mart[26], **3)**Mc Donalds[27], **4)**Microsoft[28], **5)**Mitsubishi[29], **6)**Mitsui[30], **7)**Samsung[18], **8)**Hyundai[31], **9)**Daimler-Benz[32], **10)**BMW[33], **11)** British Petroleum[34], **12)**Carefour[35] and **13)**Nestle[36]. Yes, There are 4 US, 2 Japanese, 2 Korean, 2 Germany, 1 Britain, 1 French and 1 Swiss *famous giant* <u>global world-wide</u> group of companies.

The-26 Samsung's ***IFRS*'** (*International Finance Reporting Standard*'s) ratios consist of 13 financial architecture <u>key-piles</u>[37] and 13 others <u>locked-stones</u>[38]. The-13 <u>key-piles</u> are:

    **c**= Current ratio= (**C/X**)

    **d**= Dividend paid portion to after tax = (**D/A**)

    **f**= Fix expenses portion to revenue= (**F/S**)

    **g**= Goods or trade account payable days= (360**G/V**)

    **i**= Investment or financial portion to revenue= (**I/S**)

    **j**= Job or trade account receivable days= (360**J/S**)

    **l**= Leverage or gearing = debt equity ratio

        = *DER*= (**L/E**)

    **p**= Procurred inventory days= (360**P/V**)

    **q**= Quick or acid test ratio= (**C-P**)/**X**

    **s**= Sales or revenue growth to previous = (**S/S'**-1)

    **t**= Tax rate or portion to before tax earnings= (**T/B**)

    **v**= Variable expenses portion to revenue= (**V/S**)

    **y**= Yielding tax of the dividend paid= (**Y/D**)

# Financial *Orthogonality*[39] *&Geodethical*[40] *Engineering*

If just number of financial items are harder to seen, herewith we provide also its proportional analysis using 13 key piles to define its financial structure. Since it did not pay the dividend in the 2 (two) periods, its dividend paid up ration (**d**) and yielding tax of dividend (**y**) not yet applied.

|   | 2009 | 2008 | (+) | (%) |
|---|------|------|-----|-----|
| c | 72.91% | 79.07% | -6.16% | -7.78% |
| d | 0.00% | 0.00% | 0.00% | #DIV/0! |
| f | 11.59% | 15.92% | -4.33% | -27.20% |
| g | 25.18 | 15.52 | 9.66 | 62.22% |
| i | 0.14% | 0.07% | 0.07% | 101.66% |
| j | 25.23 | 15.25 | 9.98 | 65.46% |
| l | 28.73% | 24.79% | 3.94% | 15.90% |
| p | 19.13 | 24.82 | (5.69) | -22.93% |
| q | 50.95% | 46.50% | 4.46% | 9.59% |
| s | 23.06% | | | |
| t | 11.00% | 6.47% | 4.52% | 69.92% |
| v | 76.20% | 75.91% | 0.28% | 0.37% |
| y | #DIV/0! | #DIV/0! | #DIV/0! | #DIV/0! |

As important financial architecture measures, those-13 (thirteen key piles) could be modified and determining all the remaining 13 (thirteen) other financial ratios and the 25 (twenty five) financial items except utilized equity known at the beginning of the operational year (**U**).

# Accounting's *Geology*[41] and *Soil Mechanics*[42]

Supposing that all finace architecture ratio already in place, the orthogonality in flatness of geodethical principle shape its topology, as followed by the key-piles ratio. Those finance architecture surface shape and distributed to fincace architecture locked-stones as follow:

|   | 2009 | 2008 | (+) | (%) |
|---|---|---|---|---|
| a | 11.22% | 7.62% | 3.60% | 47.20% |
| b | 12.60% | 8.15% | 4.46% | 54.68% |
| e | 14.44% | 9.51% | 4.93% | 51.85% |
| h | 0.00% | 0.00% | 0.00% | #DIV/0! |
| k | 12.94% | 20.14% | -7.19% | -35.72% |
| m | 104.36% | 100.60% | 3.76% | 3.74% |
| n | 10.75% | 7.57% | 3.17% | 41.90% |
| o | 12.75% | 8.22% | 4.53% | 55.14% |
| r | 11.22% | 7.62% | 3.60% | 47.20% |
| u | 16.88% | 10.51% | 6.37% | 60.60% |
| w | (19.17) | (24.54) | 5.37 | -21.89% |
| x | 86.20% | 81.37% | 4.83% | 5.94% |
| z | 61.28% | 64.79% | -3.51% | -5.42% |

Like in common architecture, the locked-stone in finance architecture are placed between the key piles. Together the permanent and movable components support the existing and future financial architecture building.

# CHAPTER-II: Finance *Structure Engineering*[43]

The facts those we found, could be <u>re-constructed</u> for making the <u>better finance architecture</u> building. Please see what finance architecture improvement can be made.

|   | 2010 | 2009 | (+) | (%) |
|---|---|---|---|---|
| c | 140.00% | 72.91% | 67.09% | 92.01% |
| d | 30.00% | 0.00% | 30.00% | #DIV/0! |
| f | 15.00% | 11.59% | 3.41% | 29.42% |
| g | 30.00 | 25.18 | 4.82 | 19.13% |
| i | 5.00% | 0.14% | 4.86% | 3519.88% |
| j | 15.00 | 25.23 | (10.23) | -40.54% |
| l | 100.00% | 28.73% | 71.27% | 248.06% |
| p | 15.00 | 19.13 | (4.13) | -21.57% |
| q | 100.00% | 50.95% | 49.05% | 96.25% |
| s | 30.00% | 23.06% | 6.94% | 30.12% |
| t | 30.00% | 11.00% | 19.00% | 172.84% |
| v | 70.00% | 76.20% | -6.20% | -8.13% |
| y | 20.00% | #DIV/0! | #DIV/0! | #DIV/0! |

On <u>reversing direction</u> we can set Paccioli's <u>Double entry</u> accounting back. If they start from drafts, evidences, invoices untul <u>composing</u> their Income Statement and Balance-sheet, then taking some of its proportional ratio for <u>analysis</u>. So by finance architecture we could <u>synthesize</u> it back, to <u>re-contruct</u> better <u>finance architecture</u> in <u>blue-print</u>.

# Financial *Bore Piling*[44]: *Penetration*[45] and *Erection*[46]

Paccioli will be <u>very happy</u>. Fra *Luca* Bartolomeo de *Pacioli*,[47] also called Paciolo July 1446, Sansepolcro), Italian mathematician and Franciscan friar, <u>Lucas Pacioli</u>. (Paciuolo), born at Borgo San Sepolco, Tuscany, toward the middle of the fifteenth century; died probably soon after 1509 or 1517. He establish <u>dual entry system</u>, as one of the <u>great contribution</u> to economic and finance.

|   | 2010 | 2009 | (+) | (%) |
|---|------|------|-----|-----|
| a | 5.63% | 11.22% | -5.59% | -49.80% |
| b | 8.04% | 12.60% | -4.56% | -36.17% |
| e | 7.88% | 14.44% | -6.56% | -45.41% |
| h | 2.93% | 0.00% | 2.93% | #DIV/0! |
| k | 42.86% | 12.94% | 29.91% | 231.13% |
| m | 80.44% | 104.36% | -23.92% | -22.92% |
| n | 4.90% | 10.75% | -5.85% | -54.41% |
| o | 12.07% | 12.75% | -0.68% | -5.34% |
| r | 3.94% | 11.22% | -7.28% | -64.86% |
| u | 8.56% | 16.88% | -8.32% | -49.29% |
| w | - | (19.17) | 19.17 | -100.00% |
| x | 11.73% | 86.20% | -74.47% | -86.39% |
| z | 2.35% | 61.28% | -58.93% | -96.17% |

What can we celebrate today is that the finance architecture is a <u>reversing process</u> to construct <u>desired state</u>.

# Magic Accounting *Foundations* and Financial *Pillars*[48]

Congratulation, we found the solution already. The problem of our economic teaching today, is that Pacioli's law is normally taught in algebraic method (like T-account, etc.), that are hard to be balanced. Those makes finance student (who are commonly weak in mathematics), get a headache. They then think that finance is difficult. No!

| 116,705 | 81,693 | | | | | |
|---|---|---|---|---|---|---|
| latest | 35,011 | 17,506 | | | | |
| | | 17,506 | 5,835 | | | |
| | | | 11,670 | 3,501 | | |
| | | | | 8,169 | 2,451 | 490 |
| previous | | | | | | 1,961 |
| 89,773 | | | | | 5,719 | |

**Samsung-10**

| 3,647 | 11,914 | 145,087 | 72,544 | 8,510 | 6,808 |
|---|---|---|---|---|---|
| 4,863 | | | | | 1,702 |
| 3,404 | | | | 64,034 | |
| | 133,173 | | 72,544 | 66,825 | |
| | | | | 5,719 | |

A magic comes from using geometry, of John Napier's[49] (Lord Kelvin's) idea. Napier bones had made the assumed impossible, becomes possible and be beneficial!

# Financial *Beams*[50] and *Catilever*[51] *Mechanics*

Although the finance architecture deal with many complex paper calculations, it is still much easier than exponential addition techniques. Same logic used, simplify Income Statement's mathematics. Look its improvement:

|   | 2010 | 2009 | (+) | (%) |
|---|-------|------|-----|-----|
| A | 8,169 | 9,649 | (1,480) | -15.33% |
| B | 11,670 | 10,841 | 829 | 7.65% |
| C | 11,914 | 12,067 | (153) | -1.27% |
| D | 2,451 | - | 2,451 | #DIV/0! |
| E | 72,544 | 66,825 | 5,719 | 8.56% |
| F | 17,506 | 10,405 | 7,101 | 68.24% |
| G | 6,808 | 4,785 | 2,023 | 42.27% |
| H | 1,961 | - | 1,961 | #DIV/0! |
| I | 5,835 | 124 | 5,711 | 4605.84% |
| J | 3,404 | 6,291 | (2,887) | -45.89% |
| K | 4,863 | 2,142 | 2,721 | 127.02% |
| L | 72,544 | 19,199 | 53,344 | 277.84% |
| M | 35,011 | 21,370 | 13,641 | 63.83% |

Placing these financial posts will be much easier to be done by the wole Samsung company. These numbers could be understood by all people in the organization, than just stating *ROE*, *ROA* etc, which are very difficult to be translated to reality (even by accountant). That's why the financial performance always disappointing to all parties.

# Accounting *Portals*[52] and *Vectoral*[53] *Resultants*

Could you tell us, from <u>where does the calculation</u> resulting the financial ratio said above? You will get much skill if you try to really search of where they comes from.

|   | 2010 | 2009 | (+) | (%) |
|---|---|---|---|---|
| N | 133,173 | 73,957 | 59,216 | 80.07% |
| O | 17,506 | 10,965 | 6,541 | 59.65% |
| P | 3,404 | 3,634 | (230) | -6.33% |
| Q | 64,034 | 2,649 | 61,384 | 2316.88% |
| R | 5,719 | 9,649 | (3,930) | -40.73% |
| S | 116,705 | 89,773 | 26,932 | 30.00% |
| T | 3,501 | 1,192 | 2,309 | 193.72% |
| U | 66,825 | 57,176 | 9,649 | 16.88% |
| V | 81,693 | 68,403 | 13,290 | 19.43% |
| W | 145,087 | 86,024 | 59,063 | 68.66% |
| X | 8,510 | 16,550 | (8,040) | -48.58% |
| Y | 490 | - | 490 | #DIV/0! |
| Z | 1,702 | 11,765 | (10,063) | -85.53% |

<u>Proof</u> of the pudding is the eating. To know <u>how big knowledge</u> you get here, test any <u>world finance professor</u> or <u>financial experts</u>. Just give them the <u>original Samsung 2009/2008</u> financial statement and the <u>targeted 13 (thirteen) desired key-piles</u>. Ask them their plan for end of 2010 Income Statement and Balance-sheet! *What's the answer?*

# Examinng the 13 World Famed Companies' *Basement*[54]

Finance architecture is a <u>nicer</u> but <u>simple</u> greater composition of <u>geometric finance</u> elements, visualizing the <u>Paccioli's accounting greatness</u>, by employing the boxes of <u>Napier bone's</u> geometric superiority. *It becomes very easy!*

Let's use the kindergarten or 1$^{st}$ grade algebra to realize fantastic advancement of <u>Napier-Paccioli's method</u>. Please consider the 5 (five) most common problems in very <u>fundamental algebra</u>: 3+4=?, 3+?=7, ?+4=7, 7-3=?, 7-4=? Do you familiar with them? Sure, but in Napier's geometry those are just 1 (one) case, not seen as 5(five). How comes? People mostly think them as abstract problems. Visually by Napier's box system, it can easily be drawn as simple as:

| 7 | 4 |
|---|---|
|   | 3 |

Back to the <u>Poincare's trivial</u> the 3+4=7 is a single natural fact, so then we can always find the missing one, if and only if the other two clearly identified. There are so many <u>Paccioli's boxes</u> in million of world accounting thick books, that are <u>not yet</u> presented as <u>proper by visuals</u>. The absent of Napier-Paccioli's geometric, makes the finance and accounting <u>looks difficult</u>. So then make the what Mc Kinsey[55] said as finance architecture, become just ideas and numbers, which is <u>even worse</u> than what Paccioli had set.

People better works for the <u>real number control</u>, rather than just talk about many thing that they do not able. Our world need better thinker whose makes the complex things easy. It's already too many people charging others highly, just because can make <u>simple things</u> <u>looks difficult</u> and much <u>more complicated</u> than they <u>really</u> are. *So cruel!*

# CHAPTER-III: The Paccioli's *Civil Engineering*[56]

All of the 13 world's architecture *skyscraper*[17]. (Boeing[21], Wal-Mart[22], Mc Donalds[23], Microsoft[24], Mitsubishi[25], Mitsui[26], Samsung[27], Hyundai[28], Daimler-Benz[29], BMW[30], British Petroleum[31], Carefour[32] and Nestle[33]), had been widely famous as *titans*[57] among the global world-wide companies. Yes, they are really big. What are the core of it? Sure, their profitability! Wher are them? Sure, at the right bottom (Southeast) of their balance sheet. It's their equity *Napier-Paccioli*'s box.

| E | U |
|---|---|
|   | R |

$E = (U+R)$, The ending equity ($E$) is the retained earnings ($R$), added to its utilized equity at beninning ($U$).

Using the same Napier-Paccioli's box approach, we can mearure its common $e = ROE =$ return on equity$= (R/E)$ and also u= Utilized equity return$= (R/U)$. The e=ROE had been famous worls wide assumed as the profitability measure, but now we see that $u=(R/U)$ is better, because its starting equity is $U$, not $E$ (its ending equity). $E=(U+R)$ shows that famous $e=ROE=(R/E)$ is not a proper measure of equity profitability, because has anachronic time faults.[58]

How can we find that fault easily, while thousands of finance experts in hundreds of years got wrong always? Right, because they do not use /employ Napier-Paccioli's box finance geometric (just an element of finance architecture) approach.

It's like a blind five men seeing an elephant[59] tale. The story tells that without using visual: even world's most honest, smartest, dedicated and life experienced will false. People who got profits in doing wrong way, *will not learn*!

# Nestle's Accounting *Joists*[60] and Financial *Takabeyas*[61]

Netle's financial architecture for end of 2010 could be improved by blue print of *joist* and *Takabeya*'s system:

|   | 2010 | 2009 | (+) | (%) |
|---|---|---|---|---|
| c | 140.00% | 63.12% | 76.88% | 121.79% |
| d | 30.00% | 11.64% | 18.36% | 157.68% |
| f | 35.00% | 43.92% | -8.92% | -20.30% |
| g | 120.00 | 103.78 | 16.22 | 15.62% |
| i | 5.00% | 0.74% | 4.26% | 577.70% |
| j | 30.00 | 41.18 | (11.18) | -27.14% |
| l | 100.00% | 106.81% | -6.81% | -6.38% |
| p | 60.00 | 61.59 | (1.59) | -2.58% |
| q | 100.00% | 41.69% | 58.31% | 139.87% |
| s | 20.00% | -2.08% | 22.08% | -1059.90% |
| t | 30.00% | 17.85% | 12.15% | 68.09% |
| v | 40.00% | 42.01% | -2.01% | -4.78% |
| y | 30.00% | 0.00% | 30.00% | #DIV/0! |

Nestle must and could seriously improve its internal joist on *liquidity problem*, its *bad* quick or acid test (**q**) of 41.69% could be managed to be **100%** also its current ratio ( **c**) can be handled to be **140%** from existing 63.12%. At its Takabeya, *poor* sales or revenue growth (**s**) must and can be improved to **20%** from the negative 2.08% now, and its fix expenses (f) must and can be managed to be always less than **35%** from the dangerous 43.92% of its revenue!

# The *Pyramids*[62] and *Great-wall*[63] of Nestle Accounting

If Nestle's finance architecture contractor can really manage its 2010 according the blue print, its finance result:

| | | | | | | |
|---|---|---|---|---|---|---|
| 129,142 | 51,657 | | | | | |
| latest | 77,485 | 45,200 | | | | |
| | | 32,285 | 6,457 | | | |
| | | | 25,828 | 7,748 | | |
| | | | | 18,080 | 5,424 | 1,627 |
| | | | | | | 3,797 |
| previous | | | | | | |
| 107,618 | | | | | 12,656 | |

**Nestle-10**

| | | | | | |
|---|---|---|---|---|---|
| 10,762 | 30,133 | 132,574 | 66,287 | 21,524 | 17,219 |
| 10,762 | | | | | 4,305 |
| 8,609 | | | | 44,763 | |
| | 102,441 | | 66,287 | 53,631 | |
| | | | | 12,656 | |

Its Income Statement managing the permanent sales grow (**s**) money flow like the great Chinese wall protecting the country and its improved quick or acid test (**q**) and its current (**c**) ratio make it stable as Egyptian pyramid at Giza.

Please carefully look at our 2010 Nestle's finance architecture plan. It is better than any other expert advices because it is multi constraints and comprehensively meet the 13 financial measured on finance joist and Takabeya. So then it not onle met all the-13 criteria, but it is also very realistic and not making radical difference in company acts.

# The Nestle Financial *Mastaba*[64], *Pailu*[65] and *Tori*[66]

The Nestle finance architecture is a sacred protected *place*, with managed *streams* and monumental *gate* ways:

|   | 2010 | 2009 | (+) | (%) |
|---|------|------|-----|-----|
| a | 13.64% | 10.63% | 3.01% | 28.26% |
| b | 19.48% | 12.94% | 6.54% | 50.53% |
| e | 19.09% | 19.43% | -0.34% | -1.73% |
| h | 7.08% | 0.00% | 7.08% | #DIV/0! |
| k | 50.00% | 7.58% | 42.42% | 559.89% |
| m | 97.41% | 97.03% | 0.38% | 0.40% |
| n | 9.80% | 9.68% | 0.12% | 1.21% |
| o | 24.35% | 13.66% | 10.69% | 78.30% |
| r | 9.55% | 9.39% | 0.15% | 1.62% |
| u | 23.60% | 24.11% | -0.52% | -2.14% |
| w | 30.00 | 1.02 | 28.98 | 2837.39% |
| x | 32.47% | 62.99% | -30.52% | -48.45% |
| z | 6.49% | 40.24% | -33.74% | -83.86% |

Please remember again that in finance architecture, its 13 (thirteen) *Mastaba*, *Pailu* and *Torii* are <u>locked-stones</u>, not <u>key-piles</u>, like the other end of 2010 financial measures described before, but together it construct the detail of 26 finance architecture elements of **A-Z** of the Nestle's 2010.

What important is that proportional financial ratios in finance architecture <u>must be set in advance</u>, so then the company could be <u>managed to perform</u> well as planned.

# Nestle's Financial *Hypars*[67] and *Folding Plate*[68] Roof

These are <u>extremely difficult</u>, the data tell us about future of our year or operations in their 2010 architecture:

|   | 2010 | 2009 | (+) | (%) |
|---|---|---|---|---|
| A | 18,080 | 11,793 | 6,287 | 53.31% |
| B | 25,828 | 14,355 | 11,473 | 79.93% |
| C | 30,133 | 22,777 | 7,356 | 32.30% |
| D | 5,424 | 1,373 | 4,051 | 295.04% |
| E | 66,287 | 53,631 | 12,656 | 23.60% |
| F | 45,200 | 47,261 | (2,061) | -4.36% |
| G | 17,219 | 13,033 | 4,186 | 32.12% |
| H | 3,797 | - | 3,797 | #DIV/0! |
| I | 6,457 | 794 | 5,663 | 713.23% |
| J | 8,609 | 12,309 | (3,700) | -30.06% |
| K | 10,762 | 2,734 | 8,028 | 293.63% |
| L | 66,287 | 57,285 | 9,002 | 15.71% |
| M | 77,485 | 62,410 | 15,075 | 24.15% |

The 2009 data is the base of the 13 (thirteen) finance architecture elements of Nestle Swiss. The reason that we must put the <u>hypar</u> and <u>folding plate</u> financial items as Nestle's target, is to be better understood by all the employeeand business supporters of Nestle. Normal (non visual nor items set), <u>financial ratio planning</u> will always <u>fail</u> , because only understood by finance guy who are not related (must be <u>independent</u> ) from <u>company operations</u>.

# Nestle's Finance *Pre-stress*[69] and *Tensional Cables*[70]

Although hated by economist and finance experts' Paccioli's finance geometry are interactive each to another:

|   | 2010 | 2009 | (+) | (%) |
|---|---|---|---|---|
| N | 102,441 | 88,139 | 14,302 | 16.23% |
| O | 32,285 | 15,149 | 17,136 | 113.12% |
| P | 8,609 | 7,734 | 875 | 11.32% |
| Q | 44,763 | 21,202 | 23,561 | 111.13% |
| R | 12,656 | 10,420 | 2,236 | 21.46% |
| S | 129,142 | 107,618 | 21,524 | 20.00% |
| T | 7,748 | 2,562 | 5,186 | 202.44% |
| U | 53,631 | 43,211 | 10,420 | 24.11% |
| V | 51,657 | 45,208 | 6,449 | 14.26% |
| W | 132,574 | 110,916 | 21,658 | 19.53% |
| X | 21,524 | 36,083 | (14,559) | -40.35% |
| Y | 1,627 | - | 1,627 | #DIV/0! |
| Z | 4,305 | 23,050 | (18,745) | -81.32% |

That is the reason why (even for the world's great finance professor as <u>Damodaran</u>) *fail*. <u>Sensitifity analysis</u> always works partial (usually just on <u>one element</u>). Two is difficult, threee already cheated every where and four items preset is really impossible. *Now* we had control <u>13 items!</u>

It is not because we are smarter than him, but we are more creative trained architects who improve Paccioli's <u>geometric finance</u> to <u>Napier-Paccioli</u> *finance architecture*.

# The *Zeitgeist*[71] and *Weltanschauung*[72] of Nestle Finance

Nestle finance did not started from scratch, sure it has its vision had historical back-ground and spirit of time

| 107,618 | 45,208 | | | | | |
|---|---|---|---|---|---|---|
| latest | 62,410 | 47,261 | | | | |
| | | 15,149 | 794 | | | |
| | | | 14,355 | 2,562 | | |
| | | | | 11,793 | 1,373 | - |
| | | | | | | - |
| previous | | | | | | |
| 109,908 | | | | | 10,420 | |

**Nestle-09**

| 2,734 | 22,777 | 110,916 | 57,285 | 36,083 | 13,033 |
|---|---|---|---|---|---|
| 12,309 | | | | | 23,050 |
| 7,734 | | | | 21,202 | |
| | 88,139 | | 53,631 | 43,211 | |
| | | | | 10,420 | |

Nothing wrong found in traditional or conventional accounting and finance ideas. Only 2 (two) things changes: 1) The use of finance architecture as its terminology inviting more architects and mathematical engineers to make accountancy and its economic finance be more beneficial. 2) Crowds of long and complex ineffective algebra invites geometric and algebra mathematician to make it nicer, easier and more effective to managed. Sure, some low class mathematician who get profits in finance now must respecting public right to see the truth of it.

# Monumentality[73] and Collosal[74] Heritage of Nestle

Nice works done by Nestle's management from 2008 to 2009 must be repected, they done a good job:

| 109,908 | 47,339 | | | | | |
|---|---|---|---|---|---|---|
| latest | 62,569 | 39,489 | | | | |
| | | 23,080 | 1,247 | | | |
| | | | 21,833 | 2,782 | | |
| | | | | 19,051 | 412 | - |
| previous | | | | | | - |
| - | | | | | 18,639 | |

**Nestle-08**

| 5,835 | 28,619 | 106,215 | 51,299 | 33,640 | 15,383 |
|---|---|---|---|---|---|
| 13,442 | | | | | 18,257 |
| 9,342 | | | | 17,659 | |
| 77,596 | | | 54,916 | 36,277 | |
| | | | | 18,639 | |

Remember story of five blind men and elephant? Certainly, if they can do wonderful things without visuals, can you imagine what magic the can do if the work it by visuals? Here is the finance architecture for their vision.

Although this visual method has significantly simplifying the pages of financial statements all in just half page visuals, some mathematician still need tables.

Now we also give them tables which is for experts since they just for expert, because they work with numbers, regardless the position of the items in financial statement.

# Finance *Macrocosmic* and *Microcosmic*[75] of Nestle

Like in other architecture, the finance architecture must understand where's Nestle place along its history:

|   | 2009 | 2008 | (+) | (%) |
|---|---|---|---|---|
| A | 11,793 | 19,051 | (7,258) | -38.10% |
| B | 14,355 | 21,833 | (7,478) | -34.25% |
| C | 22,777 | 28,619 | (5,842) | -20.41% |
| D | 1,373.00 | 412.00 | 961 | 233.25% |
| E | 53,631 | 54,916 | (1,285) | -2.34% |
| F | 47,261 | 39,489 | 7,772 | 19.68% |
| G | 13,033 | 15,383 | (2,350) | -15.28% |
| H | - | - | - | #DIV/0! |
| I | 794 | 1,247 | (453) | -36.33% |
| J | 12,309 | 13,442 | (1,133) | -8.43% |
| K | 2,734 | 5,835 | (3,101) | -53.14% |
| L | 57,285 | 51,299 | 5,986 | 11.67% |
| M | 62,410 | 62,569 | (159) | -0.25% |

*Nestlé* is a Nutrition, Health and Wellness company committed to increasing the <u>nutritional value</u> of our food while improving the taste,  is the <u>largest nutrition and foods</u> company <u>in the world</u>. The business already good, now if by better <u>finance architecture</u> understanding, can you imagine how good thay are, if they really can improve their debt and <u>liquidity management</u> and their <u>fix cost efficiency</u>? Wonderful the owners and investors be happier!

# Nestle Financial *Energies*[76] and *Gravitational*[77] Fields

The company with debt liquidity and fix expense problem will also suffer is sales or revenue growth (**s**):

|   | 2009 | 2008 | (+) | (%) |
|---|---|---|---|---|
| N | 88,139 | 77,596 | 10,543 | 13.59% |
| O | 15,149 | 23,080 | (7,931) | -34.36% |
| P | 7,734 | 9,342 | (1,608) | -17.21% |
| Q | 21,202 | 17,659 | 3,543 | 20.06% |
| R | 10,420 | 18,639 | (8,219) | -44.10% |
| S | 107,618 | 109,908 | (2,290) | -2.08% |
| T | 2,562 | 2,782.00 | (220) | -7.91% |
| U | 43,211 | 36,277 | 6,934 | 19.11% |
| V | 45,208 | 47,339 | (2,131) | -4.50% |
| W | 110,916 | 106,215 | 4,701 | 4.43% |
| X | 36,083 | 33,640 | 2,443 | 7.26% |
| Y | - | - | - | #DIV/0! |
| Z | 23,050 | 18,257 | 4,793 | 26.25% |

It had already happen to Nestle 2009 compared to 2008 revenue, sure it is still a big food an nutrition (consumer good) company, it also had many loyal customer world wide. That is the strength and opportunity.

How about difficulties to pay current debt? How can it handle the extra big portion of its fixed expenses? Employing stricter procedures and reducing it's material, will not help. Better finance understanding is needed here!

# Nestle's *Decomposition*[78] and Financial *Bones*[79]

Like phoenix raised from its ashes[80], Nestle would have a glorious eternal life, if it rebirth and be better:

|   | 2009 | 2008 | (+) | (%) |
|---|---|---|---|---|
| c | 63.12% | 85.07% | -21.95% | -25.80% |
| d | 11.64% | 2.16% | 9.48% | 438.35% |
| f | 43.92% | 35.93% | 7.99% | 22.23% |
| g | 103.78 | 116.98 | (13.20) | -11.28% |
| i | 0.74% | 1.13% | -0.40% | -34.97% |
| j | 41.18 | 44.03 | (2.85) | -6.48% |
| l | 106.81% | 93.41% | 13.40% | 14.34% |
| p | 61.59 | 71.04 | (9.46) | -13.31% |
| q | 41.69% | 57.30% | -15.61% | -27.25% |
| s | -2.08% | | | |
| t | 17.85% | 12.74% | 5.11% | 40.07% |
| v | 42.01% | 43.07% | -1.06% | -2.47% |
| y | 0.00% | 0.00% | 0.00% | #DIV/0! |

Finance architecture not just help it rebirth, but also thell how could it be better and really achieved that. Nestle will always face a different zeitgeist condition and should always have the proper weltanschauung to lead its ages.

Hopefully their French speakers don't mad with our Germanic expression. It isn't because the German language is more beautiful than the French one, but because those two Germanic expression had used widely in architecture.

# Financial *Turbulences*[81] and *Storms*[82] at Nestle

Situation might change, even static bridges or buildings must facing undesirable condition, so did Nestle:

|   | 2009 | 2008 | (+) | (%) |
|---|---|---|---|---|
| a | 10.63% | 17.94% | -7.30% | -40.72% |
| b | 12.94% | 20.56% | -7.61% | -37.04% |
| e | 19.43% | 33.94% | -14.51% | -42.76% |
| h | 0.00% | 0.00% | 0.00% | #DIV/0! |
| k | 7.58% | 17.35% | -9.77% | -56.32% |
| m | 97.03% | 103.48% | -6.45% | -6.23% |
| n | 9.68% | 16.96% | -7.28% | -42.91% |
| o | 13.66% | 21.73% | -8.07% | -37.15% |
| r | 9.39% | 17.55% | -8.15% | -46.47% |
| u | 24.11% | 51.38% | -27.27% | -53.07% |
| w | 1.02 | 1.91 | (0.89) | -46.56% |
| x | 62.99% | 65.58% | -2.59% | -3.95% |
| z | 40.24% | 35.59% | 4.65% | 13.06% |

Off course, we do not want the bad thing to happen, but we must prepare for the worst if it really come. Nestle had proven their strengths to stand still in <u>bad liquidity</u>, <u>high fix expenses</u> and even <u>negative revenue growth</u>.

It <u>should improve</u> its future <u>finance architecture</u>. So, never trust any finance architect who are not good in visual. <u>If they see reality</u> and <u>Nestle don't</u>, it can be a perceptual problem. How if the <u>non visual</u> finance architect is <u>blind</u>?

If in common architecture we recognize dams, bridges, *pond*, canal and water gates, same thing also implied in finance architecture. The first is the permanent money flow. It is the retained earnings ( **R**), coming from total sales or revenue (**S**) whin in Napier-Paccioli looks:

| S | (S-R) |
|---|-------|
|   | R     |

Are really familiar with our finance architecture? Here is a simplified Napier-Paccioli's Income Statement:

| S | V | (S-R) |
|---|---|-------|
|   | F |       |
|   | I |       |
|   | T |       |
|   | Y |       |
|   | H |       |
|   |   | R     |

If **S** is the total money inflow and **R** is the total money retained, then it leakage as big as (**S-R**)= (**V+F+I +T+Y+H**) following Paccioli's income statement rule.

Since **R** is the ending result, so the corporate permanent liquidity problem must a problem in 1 (one) of its 7 (seven) entry gates at **S, V, F, I, T, D= (Y+H)**.

Other than permanent liquidity problem, also exist managerial or debt management, which cause temporary liquidity problem of the company. Let us see Microsoft.

# Microsoft Accounting *Surfaces*[84] and *Viscosities*[85]

Microsoft liquidity <u>problem is deeper</u> than Nestle, not only it has the decrease in sales, and debt management, it has also the receivables (**J**) and inventory (**P**) troubles:

|   | 2010 | 2009 | (+) | (%) |
|---|-------|------|-----|-----|
| c | 110.00% | 66.53% | 43.47% | 65.35% |
| d | 20.00% | 0.00% | 20.00% | #DIV/0! |
| f | 40.00% | 45.28% | -5.28% | -11.66% |
| g | 120.00 | 98.45 | 21.55 | 21.89% |
| i | 5.00% | 0.00% | 5.00% | #DIV/0! |
| j | 60.00 | 68.95 | (8.95) | -12.98% |
| l | 100.00% | 96.90% | 3.10% | 3.20% |
| p | 40.00 | 21.24 | 18.76 | 88.36% |
| q | 100.00% | 63.88% | 36.12% | 56.56% |
| s | 10.00% | -3.28% | 13.28% | -404.69% |
| t | 30.00% | 26.50% | 3.50% | 13.22% |
| v | 20.00% | 20.80% | -0.80% | -3.85% |
| y | 30.00% | #DIV/0! | #DIV/0! | #DIV/0! |

Sure, Microsoft is also a <u>famous</u> company, but sells <u>less stable goods</u> compared to Nestle's <u>nutrients and food</u>. Technological product life cycle <u>runs faster</u> than consumer goods and <u>saturation trap</u> dangerously awaiting at future.

Its technological fixed expenses of <u>45.28%</u> is even greater than re-sellable multi national factories' of Nestle, which are just <u>43.92%</u>. *It's a finance architecture problem!*

# The *Archinedes' Screws*[86] on Microsoft Revenues

Herewith we show the visual of Microsoft 2010 finance architecture translated from its key-pile ratios:

| 64,281 | 12,856 | | | | | |
|---|---|---|---|---|---|---|
| latest | 51,425 | 25,712 | | | | |
| | | 25,712 | 3,214 | | | |
| | | | 22,498 | 6,749 | | |
| | | | | 15,749 | 3,150 | 945 |
| previous | | | | | | 2,205 |
| 58,437 | | | | | 12,599 | |

**Microsoft-10**

| 3,571 | 15,713 | 104,314 | 52,157 | 14,285 | 4,285 |
|---|---|---|---|---|---|
| 10,713 | | | | | 9,999 |
| 1,428 | | | | 37,872 | |
| | 88,601 | | 52,157 | 39,558 | |
| | | | | 12,599 | |

To increase its revenue, Microsoft must riding intellectual properties by <u>promoting un-famous</u> talented soft-ware engineers world wide. Microsoft will get their <u>money because the reputation</u> and they can <u>get better trust</u> because of Microsoft supremacy. So the Microsoft plays like a Noble institute: affirming less known scientist.

Like a group of <u>unbended arm tied prisoners</u>. Every person arms tied on 2 meters broughtable hard timber. Each person can not feeding their mouth themselves. The only way to survive is only by not egoistic: <u>feeding each other</u>!

# Microsoft *Transversal*[87] and *Longitudinal*[88] *Waves*

Let us make it clear that to add its sales, Microsoft must get significant royalty payment, out of nothing:

|   | 2010 | 2009 | (+) | (%) |
|---|---|---|---|---|
| a | 15.10% | 18.71% | -3.61% | -19.29% |
| b | 21.57% | 25.45% | -3.88% | -15.25% |
| e | 24.16% | 36.83% | -12.67% | -34.41% |
| h | 5.57% | 0.00% | 5.57% | #DIV/0! |
| k | 25.00% | 22.48% | 2.52% | 11.23% |
| m | 61.62% | 75.03% | -13.40% | -17.87% |
| n | 19.60% | 24.93% | -5.33% | -21.38% |
| o | 24.65% | 25.45% | -0.80% | -3.14% |
| r | 12.08% | 18.71% | -6.63% | -35.43% |
| u | 31.85% | 58.30% | -26.45% | -45.37% |
| w | 20.00 | 8.26 | 11.74 | 142.00% |
| x | 27.39% | 70.53% | -43.14% | -61.17% |
| z | 19.17% | 61.86% | -42.69% | -69.01% |

Yes, almost every software engineer in this world will be very happy to share 30% their royalty to Microsoft, if Microsoft affirm their product and sell it together.

So then Microsoft might keeping producing its product and get 100% money of that, and start taking 30% of any outside allied qualified engineer product sold. Its like the ISO certification[89] or Sunkist[90] orange endorsement business. Start get one third thing, out of nothing!

# Microsoft *Rock-filled Dams* and *Water-gates*

Finance architecture is not just determining criteria for good or bad company, it must create future architecture:

|   | 2010 | 2009 | (+) | (%) |
|---|-------|-------|---------|---------|
| A | 15,749 | 14,569 | 1,180 | 8.10% |
| B | 22,498 | 19,821 | 2,677 | 13.51% |
| C | 15,713 | 17,985 | (2,272) | -12.63% |
| D | 3,150 | - | 3,150 | #DIV/0! |
| E | 52,157 | 39,558 | 12,599 | 31.85% |
| F | 25,712 | 26,461 | (749) | -2.83% |
| G | 4,285 | 3,324 | 961 | 28.92% |
| H | 2,205 | - | 2,205 | #DIV/0! |
| I | 3,214 | - | 3,214 | #DIV/0! |
| J | 1,428 | 11,192 | (9,764) | -87.24% |
| K | 10,713 | 6,076 | 4,637 | 76.32% |
| L | 52,157 | 38,330 | 13,827 | 36.07% |
| M | 51,425 | 46,282 | 5,143 | 11.11% |

After *finance geometry* (Paccioli's box) and advance architecture (Napier-Paccioli's boxes) identified, it must utilize the actual historical potential of the company.

Finance architecture focus on result, so then not so many people know do it. Just like a common architecture, almost every body knows the Eiffel tower in Paris, France, but just few people can built it and only one or two really build it (like the Liberty Statue and World Trade Center).

# Microsoft *Bridges, Spring*-board *&Step Stones*

Suppose Microsoft get cash inflow from production and royalty cooperations it must <u>strengthen its asset quality</u> by procure more in <u>inventory</u> (**P**) and eliminating its job receivables (**J**), add its non current asssets (**N**):

|   | 2010 | 2009 | (+) | (%) |
|---|---|---|---|---|
| N | 88,601 | 59,903 | 28,698 | 47.91% |
| O | 25,712 | 19,821 | 5,891 | 29.72% |
| P | 1,428 | 717 | 711 | 99.23% |
| Q | 37,872 | 11,296 | 26,576 | 235.27% |
| R | 12,599 | 14,569 | (1,970) | -13.52% |
| S | 64,281 | 58,437 | 5,844 | 10.00% |
| T | 6,749 | 5,252 | 1,497 | 28.51% |
| U | 39,558 | 24,989 | 14,569 | 58.30% |
| V | 12,856 | 12,155 | 701 | 5.77% |
| W | 104,314 | 77,888 | 26,426 | 33.93% |
| X | 14,285 | 27,034 | (12,749) | -47.16% |
| Y | 945 | - | 945 | #DIV/0! |
| Z | 9,999 | 23,710 | (13,711) | -57.83% |

Another way to improve the finance architecture of Microsoft:on the similar <u>leverage or gearing</u> ratio (**l**), it can get more debt, but taken from <u>quoted longterm</u> one (**Q**).

The significant amount of it must be stored in kind of <u>cash</u> (**K**), just to improve its liquidity for increasing its <u>current</u> ( **c**) and <u>quick or acid test</u> ratio (**q**).

# Preserved[91] Historical Microsoft Finance Growth

It may agree or disagree with finance architecture blue print suggested, but have no choice with fact:

| 58,437 | 12,155 | | | | | |
|---|---|---|---|---|---|---|
| latest | 46,282 | 26,461 | | | | |
| | | 19,821 | - | | | |
| | | | 19,821 | 5,252 | | |
| | | | | 14,569 | - | - |
| | | | | | | - |
| previous | | | | | | |
| 60,420 | | | | 14,569 | | |

**Microsoft-09**

| 6,076 | 17,985 | 77,888 | 38,330 | 27,034 | 3,324 |
|---|---|---|---|---|---|
| 11,192 | | | | | 23,710 |
| 717 | | | | 11,296 | |
| | 59,903 | | 39,558 | 24,989 | |
| | | | | 14,569 | |

Microsoft here shown as having <u>good profitability</u> but <u>bad liquidity</u> in its debt management. Its <u>xpress debt</u> (**X**) is much greater than its <u>current assets</u> (**C**). Its debts, are mostly short-term and <u>zero trade related</u> (**Z**). *Dangerous*.

The non <u>current asset</u> item (**N**) already big, but in its current assets shown that it has to much <u>job receivables</u> (**J**) to be collected and just very few <u>procurred inventory</u> (**P**).

Is that appear clearer with the finance architecture?

# Accounting *Trigonometric*[92] for Microsoft

Liquidity influencing the corporate management and corporate management impacting the its revenue:

| 60,420 | 11,598 | | | | | |
|---|---|---|---|---|---|---|
| latest | 48,822 | 25,008 | | | | |
| | | 23,814 | - | | | |
| | | | 23,814 | 6,133 | | |
| | | | | 17,681 | - | - |
| previous | | | | | | - |
| #REF! | | | | | 17,681 | |

**Microsoft-08**

| 10,339 | 24,913 | 72,793 | 36,507 | 29,886 | 4,034 |
|---|---|---|---|---|---|
| 13,589 | | | | | 25,852 |
| 985 | | | | 6,621 | |
| 47,880 | | | 36,286 | 18,605 | |
| | | | | 17,681 | |

If the corporate faces a liquidity problem it's hard to pay its xpress debt (**X**), the problem then becomes bigger. When problems grow bigger, its current asset management also get difficult because it quickly runs in and out. It then impacting to its options of investment alternative and strategic sales promotion. Even though the condition still the same the corporate had weakened.

In normal condition the also get worse because of it. Lack of liquidity means fewer flexibilty, then finally makes its finance architecture and cash generating ability lower.

# Microsoft *Phytagorean*[93], *Sine, Cosine* and *Slopes*

It is nice and saving that Microsoft does not pay any financial charges (interest, exchange fee etc.):

|   | 2009 | 2008 | (+) | (%) |
|---|---|---|---|---|
| A | 14,569 | 17,681 | (3,112) | -17.60% |
| B | 19,821 | 23,814 | (3,993) | -16.77% |
| C | 17,985 | 24,913 | (6,928) | -27.81% |
| D | - | - | - | #DIV/0! |
| E | 39,558 | 36,286 | 3,272 | 9.02% |
| F | 26,461 | 25,008 | 1,453 | 5.81% |
| G | 3,324 | 4,034 | (710) | -17.60% |
| H | - | - | - | #DIV/0! |
| I | - | - | - | #DIV/0! |
| J | 11,192 | 13,589 | (2,397) | -17.64% |
| K | 6,076 | 10,339 | (4,263) | -41.23% |
| L | 38,330 | 36,507 | 1,823 | 4.99% |
| M | 46,282 | 48,822 | (2,540) | -5.20% |

Please examine its impact to the corporate liquidity: Microsoft just has 17,985 million USD at its current assets (**C** ) to pay the xpress debt (**X**) due of USD 27,034 millions at the end of 2009. *It's very dangerous!*

It's better committing additional quoted longterm debt (**Q**) to help its liquidity and place it on its kind of cash (**K**). Indepth study shows that majority or 23,710 out of the 27,034 million USD are zero trade related debts (**Z**).

# Microsoft *Platonic Solids*[94] and *Weight Balancing*[95]

Please look on its current assets (**C** ), especially the procured inventory (**P**) is just USD 717 million, too small:

|   | 2009 | 2008 | (+) | (%) |
|---|------|------|-----|-----|
| N | 59,903 | 47,880 | 12,023 | 25.11% |
| O | 19,821 | 23,814 | (3,993) | -16.77% |
| P | 717 | 985 | (268) | -27.21% |
| Q | 11,296 | 6,621 | 4,675 | 70.61% |
| R | 14,569 | 17,681 | (3,112) | -17.60% |
| S | 58,437 | 60,420 | (1,983) | -3.28% |
| T | 5,252 | 6,133.00 | (881) | -14.36% |
| U | 24,989 | 18,605 | 6,384 | 34.31% |
| V | 12,155 | 11,598 | 557 | 4.80% |
| W | 77,888 | 72,793 | 5,095 | 7.00% |
| X | 27,034 | 29,886 | (2,852) | -9.54% |
| Y | - | - | - | #DIV/0! |
| Z | 23,710 | 25,852 | (2,142) | -8.29% |

Yes, it's truly a technological company, which does not have physical inventory, but it had too much place it on the <u>fixed expenses</u> (**F**) of 26,461 million USD. It's no longer conservative, but <u>inconsistent</u> accounting records. The corporate <u>liquidity looks much poorer</u> than it as.

Learn the lesson from Edison[96], who found the light bulb on his <u>10,00 and 16,001</u> experiments. It's paid, his thousands unsuccessful experiments <u>still bring money</u>.

# Microsoft Finance *Suspension*[97] and *Stress-ringing*[98]

Here known that Microsoft's current ( **c**) and quick (**q**) ratio are in bad conditions (far  below 1.00):

|   | 2009 | 2008 | (+) | (%) |
|---|------|------|-----|-----|
| c | 66.53% | 83.36% | -16.83% | -20.19% |
| d | 0.00% | 0.00% | 0.00% | #DIV/0! |
| f | 45.28% | 41.39% | 3.89% | 9.40% |
| g | 98.45 | 125.21 | (26.77) | -21.38% |
| i | 0.00% | 0.00% | 0.00% | #DIV/0! |
| j | 68.95 | 80.97 | (12.02) | -14.84% |
| l | 96.90% | 100.61% | -3.71% | -3.69% |
| p | 21.24 | 30.57 | (9.34) | -30.54% |
| q | 63.88% | 80.06% | -16.19% | -20.22% |
| s | -3.28% | | | |
| t | 26.50% | 25.75% | 0.74% | 2.89% |
| v | 20.80% | 19.20% | 1.60% | 8.36% |
| y | #DIV/0! | #DIV/0! | #DIV/0! | #DIV/0! |

Its current assets could not pay the current liabilities and its procured inventory is very few. The difference between its current and quick ratio is just **c-q**= 2.65% (two point sixty five percent).

Its job receivable days (**j**) extremely long, and not suitable for soft technological service that are hard to be returned and re-sell. So those are not a strong collectibles that contains strong or hard value of secured money.

# Microsoft *Arches*[99], *Flying Buttresses*[100] and aqueducts[101]

Microsoft get goods payable days (**g**) longer than procured inventory days (**p**) and job receivable days(**j**):

|   | 2009 | 2008 | (+) | (%) |
|---|------|------|------|------|
| a | 18.71% | 24.29% | -5.58% | -22.99% |
| b | 25.45% | 32.71% | -7.27% | -22.21% |
| e | 36.83% | 48.73% | -11.90% | -24.42% |
| h | 0.00% | 0.00% | 0.00% | #DIV/0! |
| k | 22.48% | 34.59% | -12.12% | -35.03% |
| m | 75.03% | 83.00% | -7.98% | -9.61% |
| n | 24.93% | 29.26% | -4.33% | -14.80% |
| o | 25.45% | 32.71% | -7.27% | -22.21% |
| r | 18.71% | 24.29% | -5.58% | -22.99% |
| u | 58.30% | 95.03% | -36.73% | -38.65% |
| w | 8.26 | 13.67 | (5.41) | -39.56% |
| x | 70.53% | 81.86% | -11.33% | -13.85% |
| z | 61.86% | 70.81% | -8.96% | -12.65% |

It is clearly shown hare that Microsoft had a negative working capital days, because its supplier's credit are still longer than the time for its inventory stored added by its trade receivable days. Sure, it has a good business.

What make them difficult is the bad liability management that majority of its debts are xpress short term (**x**) and most of them are used for zero trade related usage (**z**). Those unproductive acts must be paid back quickly.

Accounting and financial landscape is the art of balancing assets and debts of the corporation.

| W | L |
|---|---|
|   | E |

Long-term wealth (**W**) asset management is easier, supposing that the Equity (**E**) is positive, then **W > L**, because **W= (E+L)** at **E** >0.

| L | X |
|---|---|
|   | Q |

In the liability (**L**) side, quoted long-term debt (**Q**) will bring better liquidity than the xpresss (**X**) one.

| X | G |
|---|---|
|   | Z |

In xpress debt (**X**) management, majority of it must consist of goods or trade payables (**G**) and only few of them in zero trade related one (**Z**).

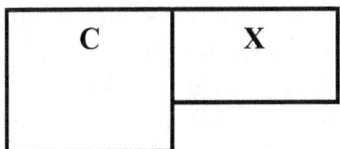

In short-term money management, its current assets ( **C**) must be greater than its xpress debts (**X**) as proper.

Mc Donalds current ( **c**) and quick (**q**) ratios both must be set to be at least 100% to better survive.

|   | 2010 | 2009 | (+) | (%) |
|---|------|------|-----|-----|
| c | 110.00% | 99.10% | 10.90% | 11.00% |
| d | 30.00% | 0.00% | 30.00% | #DIV/0! |
| f | 10.00% | 10.13% | -0.13% | -1.32% |
| g | 21.00 | 16.41 | 4.59 | 27.98% |
| i | 5.00% | 0.00% | 5.00% | #DIV/0! |
| j | 12.00 | 16.78 | (4.78) | -28.47% |
| l | 100.00% | 115.58% | -15.58% | -13.48% |
| p | 2.50 | 2.73 | (0.23) | -8.59% |
| q | 100.00% | 95.55% | 4.45% | 4.66% |
| s | 10.00% | -3.30% | 13.30% | -402.73% |
| t | 30.00% | 29.84% | 0.16% | 0.52% |
| v | 60.00% | 61.35% | -1.35% | -2.19% |
| y | 30.00% | #DIV/0! | #DIV/0! | #DIV/0! |

It has a good profitability and debt management so far, but still dangerous because both of its **c** and **q** are below 100%. Also its liability (**L**) is greater than its equity (**E**), because its l= leverage= (**L/E**) is greater than 100%.

Those liquidity matters (**c**, **q**, and **l**) impacting also on its salaes or revenue growth (**s**) and its dividend payout (**d**). To be a better company, Mc Donalds finance architecture must improve them until be bigger than 100%

# Finance *Planology*[105] on *City* and *Region* of Mc Donalds

The beauty of Mc Donal finance architecture would elaborate all its financial strengthes achieved today.

| 25,020 | 15,012 | | | | | |
|---|---|---|---|---|---|---|
| latest | 10,008 | 2,502 | | | | |
| | | 7,506 | 1,251 | | | |
| | | | 6,255 | 1,876 | | |
| | | | | 4,378 | 1,314 | 394 |
| previous | | | | | | 919 |
| 22,745 | | | | | 3,065 | |

**MacDonalds-10**

| 208 | 1,147 | 34,198 | 17,099 | 1,042 | 876 |
|---|---|---|---|---|---|
| 834 | | | | | 167 |
| 104 | | | | 16,056 | |
| | 33,051 | | 17,099 | 14,034 | |
| | | | | 3,065 | |

Its strong equity (**E**) and weak sales or revenue growth (**s**), makes it difficult to get its saler or revenue (**S**) appear greater than its wealth or total assets (**W**).

Like in the era of Ray Croc, selling burger still always difficult today, so after selling its franchise, Mc Donalds now must sell its strength in brand management.

Large property owner will sell its shops, land and houses better, if there is a Mc Donalds on its part. Mc Donalds outlet will attract many buyers and make the property a better place to live and its value increasing.

The zero trade portion (**z**) of Mc Donalds xpress liability cut drastically to make the company safer.

|   | 2010 | 2009 | (+) | (%) |
|---|---|---|---|---|
| a | 12.80% | 15.04% | -2.24% | -14.88% |
| b | 18.29% | 21.44% | -3.15% | -14.70% |
| e | 17.92% | 32.43% | -14.50% | -44.73% |
| h | 6.55% | 0.00% | 6.55% | #DIV/0! |
| k | 20.00% | 60.09% | -40.09% | -66.71% |
| m | 73.16% | 75.18% | -2.02% | -2.68% |
| n | 12.25% | 20.01% | -7.76% | -38.78% |
| o | 21.95% | 21.44% | 0.51% | 2.37% |
| r | 8.96% | 15.04% | -6.08% | -40.42% |
| u | 21.84% | 47.99% | -26.15% | -54.49% |
| w | 6.50 | (3.10) | 9.60 | -309.49% |
| x | 6.10% | 18.43% | -12.33% | -66.91% |
| z | 0.98% | 14.51% | -13.53% | -93.28% |

It has also the 5% reserve for financial expenses if needed, so then if it's used the corporate will get its profitability slightly lower, but if it did not used, its profitability will be greater than previous years.

Its kind of cash portion (k) also improved, so then Mc Donalds will have better capability to pay its xpress debt (x), which is now becomes much lower compared to its previous years. Its share holders will also get bigger dividend while their equity grow in a very secured way.

Mc Donalds should also pay its annual dividend (**D**) so then its share holder can enjoy both growth and profit.

|   | 2010 | 2009 | (+) | (%) |
|---|---|---|---|---|
| A | 4,378 | 4,551 | (173) | -3.79% |
| B | 6,255 | 6,487 | (232) | -3.58% |
| C | 1,147 | 2,962 | (1,815) | -61.29% |
| D | 1,314 | - | 1,314 | #DIV/0! |
| E | 17,099 | 14,034 | 3,065 | 21.84% |
| F | 2,502 | 2,305 | 197 | 8.54% |
| G | 876 | 636 | 240 | 37.69% |
| H | 919 | - | 919 | #DIV/0! |
| I | 1,251 | - | 1,251 | #DIV/0! |
| J | 104 | 1,060 | (956) | -90.17% |
| K | 834 | 1,796 | (962) | -53.56% |
| L | 17,099 | 16,221 | 878 | 5.41% |
| M | 10,008 | 8,792 | 1,216 | 13.83% |

Investment expenses allowance (**I**) will also makes Mc Donalds position safer, it will still survive even though it must pay unpredictably financial charges of its liquidity to cover its short term liability (**L**).

It is just in case prevention, since for 2010 Mc Donalds already suggested to maintain better liquidity or current assets to cover its huge xpress debts. Now it has much stronger current assets ( **C**) to cover its liabilities (**L**).

# Mc Donalds *Medieval Barroque*[110] vs *Rococo*[111] Finance

Elimination of unnecessary xpress debts (X) must be the priority of Mc Donalds finance architecture today.

|   | 2010 | 2009 | (+) | (%) |
|---|---|---|---|---|
| N | 33,051 | 27,293 | 5,758 | 21.10% |
| O | 7,506 | 6,487 | 1,019 | 15.71% |
| P | 104 | 106 | (2) | -1.65% |
| Q | 16,056 | 13,232 | 2,824 | 21.35% |
| R | 3,065 | 4,551 | (1,486) | -32.65% |
| S | 25,020 | 22,745 | 2,275 | 10.00% |
| T | 1,876 | 1,936 | (60) | -3.08% |
| U | 14,034 | 9,483 | 4,551 | 47.99% |
| V | 15,012 | 13,953 | 1,059 | 7.59% |
| W | 34,198 | 30,255 | 3,943 | 13.03% |
| X | 1,042 | 2,989 | (1,947) | -65.12% |
| Y | 394 | - | 394 | #DIV/0! |
| Z | 167 | 2,353 | (2,186) | -92.91% |

Greater non current assets (**N**) and greater quoted long-term debt (**Q**) will significantly improve Mc Donalds finance architecture and make its people live better.

Greater operational surplus (**O**) and legally lower tax paid (**T**) on stronger utilized equity (**U**), and lower xpress debts (**X**), makes the grow of Mc Donalds wealth or total assets (**W**) more beautiful. Its finance architecture can be more artistic and better respected world wide.

Finance Architecture of Mc Donalds 2009 traits are big profit, bad liquidity and big zero trade xpress debt (**Z**):

| 22,745 | 13,953 | | | | | |
|---|---|---|---|---|---|---|
| latest | 8,792 | 2,305 | | | | |
| | | 6,487 | - | | | |
| | | | 6,487 | 1,936 | | |
| | | | | 4,551 | - | - |
| previous | | | | | | - |
| 23,522 | | | | 4,551 | | |

**MacDonalds-09**

| 1,796 | 2,962 | 30,255 | 16,221 | 2,989 | 636 |
|---|---|---|---|---|---|
| 1,060 | | | | | 2,353 |
| 106 | | | | 13,232 | |
| | 27,293 | | 14,034 | 9,483 | |
| | | | | 4,551 | |

Aside from its good long-term and short-term debt management, its xpress debt (**X**) mostly for zero trade related items (**Z**) and just a few of them used for productive goods or trade account payables (**G**). Its current asssets ( **C**) could not cover immediate xpress debts (X) and it has only few procured inventory (**P**).

Mc Donalds is a super company with good management, but must carefully work on its current ratio ( **c**) management to be always greater than 1. Failure to pay its xpress debts (**X**), will ruin its fantastic brand image.

# Mc Donalds Basic Finance Geometric and *Key-stone*[113]

Finance architecture of Mc Donalds on 2008 shown less profitability, but better short-term debt management.

| 23,522 | 14,883 | | | | | |
|---|---|---|---|---|---|---|
| latest | 8,639 | 2,481 | | | | |
| | | 6,158 | - | | | |
| | | | 6,158 | 1,845 | | |
| | | | | 4,313 | - | - |
| previous | | | | | | - |
| - | | | | | 4,313 | |

**MacDonalds-08**

| 2,063 | 3,106 | 28,462 | 15,079 | 2,538 | 620 |
|---|---|---|---|---|---|
| 931 | | | | | 1,918 |
| 112 | | | | 12,541 | |
| 25,356 | | | 13,383 | 9,070 | |
| | | | | 4,313 | |

The zero trade debts (**Z**) still dominate its xpress current liabilities (**X**), but those are controllable since it has current assets ( **C**) bigger than them, or C>X. It has also beter kind of cash (**K**) position and stronger procured inventory (**P**) composition.

The profitability is less than its 2009 figure, but still great: a 4,313 retained earnings ( **R**), out of 23,522 sales or revenue (**S**) that starts from 9,070 utilized equity (**U**). Its areasonable great profit achieved safely in proper short-term liquidity management better than its 2009 structure.

# _Dolmen_[114] and _Megalith_ of Mc Donalds Finance

Existing Mc Donalds 2009 finance architecture is much more dangerous than its 2008 finance position.

|   | 2009 | 2008 | (+) | (%) |
|---|--------|--------|--------|---------|
| A | 4,551 | 4,313 | 238 | 5.52% |
| B | 6,487 | 6,158 | 329 | 5.34% |
| C | 2,962 | 3,106 | (144) | -4.64% |
| D | - | - | - | #DIV/0! |
| E | 14,034 | 13,383 | 651 | 4.86% |
| F | 2,305 | 2,481 | (176) | -7.09% |
| G | 636 | 620 | 16 | 2.58% |
| H | - | - | - | #DIV/0! |
| I | - | - | - | #DIV/0! |
| J | 1,060 | 931 | 129 | 13.86% |
| K | 1,796 | 2,063 | (267) | -12.94% |
| L | 16,221 | 15,079 | 1,142 | 7.57% |
| M | 8,792 | 8,639 | 153 | 1.77% |

Compared to its 2008 finance architecture, its 2009 structure is collapsing, with greater liabilities or bigger total debts (**L**), on less current assets ( **C**) and smaller kind of cash (**K**) position, where aothers things being equal (_ceteris paribus_). I can easily collapsing if does not improved now.

Mc Donald is a great company with superior brand image and good profitability, but shown here as very weak in its current assets and short-term debts management.

# Mc Donalds *Experimental*[115] *Research Based* Finance

Mc Donalds tried hard to increase its wealth or total assets (**W**), while facing less sales or revenue (**S**):

|   | 2009 | 2008 | (+) | (%) |
|---|------|------|-----|-----|
| N | 27,293 | 25,356 | 1,937 | 7.64% |
| O | 6,487 | 6,158 | 329 | 5.34% |
| P | 106 | 112 | (6) | -5.36% |
| Q | 13,232 | 12,541 | 691 | 5.51% |
| R | 4,551 | 4,313 | 238 | 5.52% |
| S | 22,745 | 23,522 | (777) | -3.30% |
| T | 1,936 | 1,845.00 | 91 | 4.93% |
| U | 9,483 | 9,070 | 413 | 4.55% |
| V | 13,953 | 14,883 | (930) | -6.25% |
| W | 30,255 | 28,462 | 1,793 | 6.30% |
| X | 2,989 | 2,538 | 451 | 17.77% |
| Y | - | - | - | #DIV/0! |
| Z | 2,353 | 1,918 | 435 | 22.68% |

This effort seems unsuccessful, and only some of them absorbed in increasing of its quoted long-term debts (**Q**), most of them must be paid quickly as additional xpress debts (**X**), and even worse than that it falls on its zero trade related xpress liabilities (**Z**). It's costly and very dangerous.

Now it must: 1) improving its finance architecture on the xpress debt (**X**) especially on its zero trade payables (**Z**) and 2) managing to rejuvenate its Sales or revenue (**S**).

# Mc Donalds *Engineering Physics*[116] for Finance

Share holders of Mc Donalds in 2009 did not recive dividend, but the company still suffering liquidity problem.

|   | 2009 | 2008 | (+) | (%) |
|---|------|------|-----|-----|
| c | 99.10% | 122.38% | -23.28% | -19.03% |
| d | 0.00% | 0.00% | 0.00% | #DIV/0! |
| f | 10.13% | 10.55% | -0.41% | -3.92% |
| g | 16.41 | 15.00 | 1.41 | 9.42% |
| i | 0.00% | 0.00% | 0.00% | #DIV/0! |
| j | 16.78 | 14.25 | 2.53 | 17.75% |
| l | 115.58% | 112.67% | 2.91% | 2.58% |
| p | 2.73 | 2.71 | 0.03 | 0.95% |
| q | 95.55% | 117.97% | -22.42% | -19.00% |
| s | -3.30% | | | |
| t | 29.84% | 29.96% | -0.12% | -0.39% |
| v | 61.35% | 63.27% | -1.93% | -3.05% |
| y | #DIV/0! | #DIV/0! | #DIV/0! | #DIV/0! |

Both its current ratio ( c) and quick ratio (q) become worse from 2008 to 2009, they both fall from above 1 to below 1, while its procured inventory days (p) increasing.

Those become a double smash for Mc Donalds, I gaves more receivables to others, while it is in bad liquidity situation for itself. The sales grow (s) drops to negative while its share holders did not get divid3end paid on 2009.

Sure, we must and can improve both problems.

# Accounting _Mendeleev's Table_[117] of Mc Donalds

Finance architecture also consist of many different elements of chemistry, which must be understood well.

|   | 2009 | 2008 | (+) | (%) |
|---|---|---|---|---|
| a | 15.04% | 15.15% | -0.11% | -0.74% |
| b | 21.44% | 21.64% | -0.19% | -0.90% |
| e | 32.43% | 32.23% | 0.20% | 0.62% |
| h | 0.00% | 0.00% | 0.00% | #DIV/0! |
| k | 60.09% | 81.28% | -21.20% | -26.08% |
| m | 75.18% | 82.64% | -7.47% | -9.03% |
| n | 20.01% | 18.34% | 1.67% | 9.12% |
| o | 21.44% | 21.64% | -0.19% | -0.90% |
| r | 15.04% | 15.15% | -0.11% | -0.74% |
| u | 47.99% | 47.55% | 0.44% | 0.92% |
| w | (3.10) | (1.96) | (1.14) | 58.23% |
| x | 18.43% | 16.83% | 1.60% | 9.48% |
| z | 14.51% | 12.72% | 1.79% | 14.04% |

Mc Donalds get its kind of cash liquidity ratio (k), xpress current debt portion (x) and market run or asset turn-over (m) worse, although its operational surplus to asset return (o) and net profit margin (n) improved.

Its marketing and operational management team performing very well, while its finance executive doing wrong, by not managing its financial performance. They do not have balanced qualified team in its finance architecture.

# CHAPTER-VI: *Public* [118]*vs Social Facility Finance*

Professional company finance architecture, in general, must consider the leverage ($l= L/E$), factor to be slightly less than 1 (one), or ($L <= E$). So then its wealth or total assets (**W**) must be slightly less than 2 times of its equity (**E**). Problem arise if **L** is greater than **E**, or ($L > E$).

| W | L |
|---|---|
|   | E |

On the short-ter liquidity management, its current assets ( **C**), or the total of: 1)Kind of cash (**K**), 2)Job or account receivables (**J**) and 3)Procurred inventory (**P**), must always be greater than its xpress debt (**X**). It's expressed at current ratio ($c= C/X$).

| K | C | X |
|---|---|---|
| J |   |   |
| P |   |   |

In normal condition, the procured inventory (**P**) is difficult to be used as a mode to pay the xpress debts (**X**), so the xpess debt (**X** must be paid just by kind of cash (**K**) and job or trade account receivables (**J**). It's the technical aspect of quick ratio ($q$)= $(C-P)/X= (K+J)/X$.

| K | X |
|---|---|
| J |   |

It seems that every body learning finance already know that prindiple

# _Obelisk[119]_ in Strategic Accounting Places of Wal-Mart

It is shown here that Wal-Mart's current ratio ( c) and quick ratio or acid test (q) must be improved quickly.

|   | 2010 | 2009 | (+) | (%) |
|---|---|---|---|---|
| c | 150.00% | 82.49% | 67.51% | 81.84% |
| d | 20.00% | 2.57% | 17.43% | 679.21% |
| f | 15.00% | 18.90% | -3.90% | -20.63% |
| g | 45.00 | 33.92 | 11.08 | 32.66% |
| i | 3.00% | 0.47% | 2.53% | 540.43% |
| j | 3.00 | 3.47 | (0.47) | -13.44% |
| l | 100.00% | 150.33% | -50.33% | -33.48% |
| p | 30.00 | 40.58 | (10.58) | -26.07% |
| q | 100.00% | 20.18% | 79.82% | 395.44% |
| s | 10.00% | 7.17% | 2.83% | 39.50% |
| t | 30.00% | 34.19% | -4.19% | -12.25% |
| v | 70.00% | 75.48% | -5.48% | -7.26% |
| y | 30.00% | 0.00% | 30.00% | #DIV/0! |

The case arose because it committing too much leverage or gearing ratio (**l**= L/E) at **L**= liabilities at total and **E**= equity at the end or its operational period.

The figure suggested for 2010 is **_SMART_**= specific, measurable, realistic and achievable. The actions can make Wal-Mart's finance architecture better and the people there will live happier, because they are no longer be collected and can manage its debt payment much better. _Simple!_

# Restoration[120] of Wal-Mart Finance Architecture

Wal-Mart shall achieve a better finance architecture for the end of 2010 after managing its leverage (**l**):

| 446,168 | 312,317 | | | | | |
|---|---|---|---|---|---|---|
| latest | 133,850 | 66,925 | | | | |
| | | 66,925 | 13,385 | | | |
| | | | 53,540 | 16,062 | | |
| | | | | 37,478 | 7,496 | 2,249 |
| | | | | | | 5,247 |
| previous | | | | | 29,982 | |
| 405,607 | | | | | | |

**Wal-Mart-10**

| 48,335 | 78,079 | 190,535 | 95,267 | 52,053 | 39,040 |
|---|---|---|---|---|---|
| 3,718 | | | | | 13,013 |
| 26,026 | | | | 43,215 | |
| | 112,456 | | 95,267 | 65,285 | |
| | | | | 29,982 | |

They still enjoying its good profitability while solving its liquidity problems. Please look at our financial plan above. Now its current assets ( **C**) is greater than its xpress debt (**X**). Even its Kind of Cash (**K**) and job receivables can perfectly covering the xpress debts (**X**).

Please also verify the proposed leverage above, now the liability at total (**L**) no longer greater than its equity (**E**).

It is a much safer finance architecture for the people living in very profitable (still) Wal-Mart mega structure. They can now enjoy profit withour taking too much risks.

# Wal-Mart *Ecliptical[121] Annual Solar Revolution*

Major changes in Wal-Mart finance architecture is just its zero trade xpress debt proportion (**z**).

|   | 2010 | 2009 | (+) | (%) |
|---|---|---|---|---|
| a | 19.67% | 8.42% | 11.25% | 133.74% |
| b | 28.10% | 12.79% | 15.31% | 119.75% |
| e | 31.47% | 20.53% | 10.95% | 53.33% |
| h | 8.04% | 0.00% | 8.04% | #DIV/0! |
| k | 92.86% | 13.13% | 79.72% | 606.99% |
| m | 234.17% | 248.19% | -14.02% | -5.65% |
| n | 6.72% | 3.30% | 3.42% | 103.41% |
| o | 35.12% | 13.95% | 21.18% | 151.80% |
| r | 15.74% | 8.20% | 7.54% | 91.92% |
| u | 45.93% | 25.83% | 20.10% | 77.82% |
| w | 12.00 | (10.12) | 22.12 | -218.53% |
| x | 54.64% | 56.44% | -1.80% | -3.19% |
| z | 13.66% | 27.04% | -13.38% | -49.49% |

Asisde from its liquidity improvement, profitability also improve signifgicantly in almost all financial measures. It makes the Wal-Mart financial architecture, a better place for living with pleasant whether for working.

Wal-Mart already a giant in shoping center and super mall management, but must learn some principle of finance architecture to improve what they already good at.

# Wal-Mart Accounting's *Azimuth, and Elevation*[122]

Finance architecture also deals with climate and earth position in supreme universe system.

|   | 2010 | 2009 | (+) | (%) |
|---|---|---|---|---|
| A | 37,478 | 13,753 | 23,725 | 172.51% |
| B | 53,540 | 20,898 | 32,642 | 156.20% |
| C | 78,079 | 45,691 | 32,388 | 70.89% |
| D | 7,496 | 353 | 7,143 | 2023.40% |
| E | 95,267 | 65,285 | 29,982 | 45.93% |
| F | 66,925 | 76,651 | (9,726) | -12.69% |
| G | 39,040 | 28,849 | 10,191 | 35.32% |
| H | 5,247 | - | 5,247 | #DIV/0! |
| I | 13,385 | 1,900 | 11,485 | 604.48% |
| J | 26,026 | 3,905 | 22,121 | 566.49% |
| K | 3,718 | 7,275 | (3,557) | -48.89% |
| L | 95,267 | 98,144 | (2,877) | -2.93% |
| M | 133,850 | 99,449 | 34,401 | 34.59% |

We prove here that almost every thing nust be and could be improved at Wal-Mart, both its profitability and liquidity matters as well. There are fix cost portion (**F**), after tax earnings (**A**), before tax earnings (**B**), dividend paid for its profitability.

We also note here that it also get strengthen in its current assets ( **C**), investment and financial charges (**I**), equity (**E**), goods or trade payables (**G**), and lianbility (**L**).

# The Financial *Planar, Zenith &Nadir*[123] of Wal-Mart

Can you see this clearly? Wal-Mart zero trade related xpress debts (**Z**) elimination will makes it better?

|   | 2010 | 2009 | (+) | (%) |
|---|------|------|-----|-----|
| N | 112,456 | 117,738 | (5,282) | -4.49% |
| O | 66,925 | 22,798 | 44,127 | 193.56% |
| P | 26,026 | 34,511 | (8,485) | -24.59% |
| Q | 43,215 | 42,754 | 461 | 1.08% |
| R | 29,982 | 13,400 | 16,582 | 123.75% |
| S | 446,168 | 405,607 | 40,561 | 10.00% |
| T | 16,062 | 7,145 | 8,917 | 124.80% |
| U | 65,285 | 51,885 | 13,400 | 25.83% |
| V | 312,317 | 306,158 | 6,159 | 2.01% |
| W | 190,535 | 163,429 | 27,106 | 16.59% |
| X | 52,053 | 55,390 | (3,337) | -6.02% |
| Y | 2,249 | - | 2,249 | #DIV/0! |
| Z | 13,013 | 26,541 | (13,528) | -50.97% |

Allocating things less in zero trade related matters (**Z**) and taking more on the or trade goods payables (**G**). The liquidity will almost be the same, but the purpose achievements are significantly different.

In the practical super market business like Wal-Mart, the **G** normally are interest free, but the **Z** are charged with high interest for its investment or financial charges. So then the visual finance architecture does help it.

# Wal-Mart *Golden Section*[124] of *Aesthetical* Finance

Finance architecture also plays with nice proportion that brings safety and artistic beauty for better living.

| | | | | | | |
|---|---|---|---|---|---|---|
| 405,607 | 306,158 | | | | | |
| latest | 99,449 | 76,651 | | | | |
| | | 22,798 | 1,900 | | | |
| | | | 20,898 | 7,145 | | |
| | | | | 13,753 | 353 | - |
| previous | | | | | | - |
| 378,476 | | | | | 13,400 | |

**Wal-Mart-09**

| | | | | | |
|---|---|---|---|---|---|
| 7,275 | 45,691 | 163,429 | 98,144 | 55,390 | 28,849 |
| 3,905 | | | | | 26,541 |
| 34,511 | | | | 42,754 | |
| | 117,738 | | 65,285 | 51,885 | |
| | | | | 13,400 | |

Sure, it is needed here. The finance architect could not control its xpress debt (**X**) to be always less than its kind of cash (**K**) and job or trade receivables (**J**). Now the **X** has already bigger that its current assets ( **C**), here is where its trouble started: did not or could not manage.

Such a pitty that even a world class corporate like this does not manage its finance architecture. It is not only bad, but it also bring danger, because of its weak structure.

Its finance officer must be better than that, they must be finance architects with solid finance blue prints.

Finance architecture innovation needed here, Wal-Mart problem already exist but didn't solved since 2008.

| | | | | | | |
|---|---|---|---|---|---|---|
| 378,476 | 286,350 | | | | | |
| latest | 92,126 | 70,174 | | | | |
| | | 21,952 | 1,794 | | | |
| | | | 20,158 | 6,889 | | |
| | | | | 13,269 | 538 | - |
| previous | | | | | | - |
| - | | | | | 12,731 | |

**Wal-Mart-08**

| | | | | | |
|---|---|---|---|---|---|
| 5,492 | 44,293 | 163,514 | 98,906 | 58,478 | 30,344 |
| 3,642 | | | | | 28,134 |
| 35,159 | | | | 40,428 | |
| | 119,221 | | 64,608 | 51,877 | |
| | | | | 12,731 | |

Its 2008 figure expressing same profitability condition, with even worse liquidity management that must be improved quickly, not because of aesthetical reasons but also to make the finance architecture be much safer to live.

This data tell us that the bad condition are not just accident, but raised as the effect of not using visual approach on finance. Without using visuals they could not differentiate tigers with cats and they face real danger quickly. They must lear finance architecture quickly, if they no longer want to live bitter again and avoid the danger.

# Accounting *Construction Management*[126] at Wal-Mart

What it shows us here is extremely bad liquidity management problem both in general and its short-term.

|   | 2009 | 2008 | (+) | (%) |
|---|---|---|---|---|
| A | 13,753 | 13,269 | 484 | 3.65% |
| B | 20,898 | 20,158 | 740 | 3.67% |
| C | 45,691 | 44,293 | 1,398 | 3.16% |
| D | 353.00 | 538.00 | (185) | -34.39% |
| E | 65,285 | 64,608 | 677 | 1.05% |
| F | 76,651 | 70,174 | 6,477 | 9.23% |
| G | 28,849 | 30,344 | (1,495) | -4.93% |
| H | - | - | - | #DIV/0! |
| I | 1,900 | 1,794 | 106 | 5.91% |
| J | 3,905 | 3,642 | 263 | 7.22% |
| K | 7,275 | 5,492 | 1,783 | 32.47% |
| L | 98,144 | 98,906 | (762) | -0.77% |
| M | 99,449 | 92,126 | 7,323 | 7.95% |

As a great retail company it can easily delay the payment to its supplier, but this seems had no longer been easy, because the good or trade payables (**g**) to its supplier had been more than 30 days long. Its problem almost with the zero trade related xpress creaditors who are in stronger bargaining power than its common hypermarket suppliers.

Leverage (**l**= **L/E**) also a problem, since it already had too much liabilities (**L**) compared to its equity (**E**).

# Wal-Mart Finance and *Value Engineering*[127]

Wal-Mart is very strong in its market run or asset turn-over (**m**), it sells two and a half times, of its assets.

|   | 2009 | 2008 | (+) | (%) |
|---|------|------|-----|-----|
| N | 117,738 | 119,221 | (1,483) | -1.24% |
| O | 22,798 | 21,952 | 846 | 3.85% |
| P | 34,511 | 35,159 | (648) | -1.84% |
| Q | 42,754 | 40,428 | 2,326 | 5.75% |
| R | 13,400 | 12,731 | 669 | 5.25% |
| S | 405,607 | 378,476 | 27,131 | 7.17% |
| T | 7,145 | 6,889.00 | 256 | 3.72% |
| U | 51,885 | 51,877 | 8 | 0.02% |
| V | 306,158 | 286,350 | 19,808 | 6.92% |
| W | 163,429 | 163,514 | (85) | -0.05% |
| X | 55,390 | 58,478 | (3,088) | -5.28% |
| Y | - | - | - | #DIV/0! |
| Z | 26,541 | 28,134 | (1,593) | -5.66% |

Although it has a very huge cash flow as the starting point, it must seriously manage its xpress debt portion (**x**) to be as small as possible, or mostly have longterm debts. Inside its current liquidity management, it must minimize its sero trade xpress debts (**z**) also be as small as possible.

Priority on long-term debts and charged free goods payable productive supplier's credit will make Wal-Mart's strengths, enable it to give the world *everyday low prices*.

# Finance *Big Bang*[128] vs *Le Maitre's Egg*[129] of Wal-Mart

The situations runs difficult while Wal-Mart increase its kind of cash (**K**) and reducing its dividend (**D**).

|   | 2009 | 2008 | (+) | (%) |
|---|------|------|-----|-----|
| c | 82.49% | 75.74% | 6.75% | 8.91% |
| d | 2.57% | 4.05% | -1.49% | -36.70% |
| f | 18.90% | 18.54% | 0.36% | 1.92% |
| g | 33.92 | 38.15 | (4.23) | -11.08% |
| i | 0.47% | 0.47% | -0.01% | -1.18% |
| j | 3.47 | 3.46 | 0.00 | 0.05% |
| l | 150.33% | 153.09% | -2.75% | -1.80% |
| p | 40.58 | 44.20 | (3.62) | -8.19% |
| q | 20.18% | 15.62% | 4.56% | 29.22% |
| s | 7.17% | | | |
| t | 34.19% | 34.18% | 0.01% | 0.04% |
| v | 75.48% | 75.66% | -0.18% | -0.23% |
| y | 0.00% | 0.00% | 0.00% | #DIV/0! |

Other things run the same way (whether for good or bad) between 2008 and 2009, but 2 (two) things changed drastically. Its **K** increasing 32.47% while its **D** dropped 34.39%, seems that it did not pay the **D** and keep it as **K**.

This was good as the liquidity buffer to solve its xpress debt and zero trade current debts, but could easily demotivate stake holders. It needs better solution that will not be found until it improves its finance architecture.

# The Wal-Mart Finance *Einstein-Planck*[130] Physics

What makes Wal-Mart stil have ample energy to pass the 2009 will all the obstacles it faced?

|   | 2009 | 2008 | (+) | (%) |
|---|------|------|-----|-----|
| a | 8.42% | 8.11% | 0.30% | 3.70% |
| b | 12.79% | 12.33% | 0.46% | 3.72% |
| e | 20.53% | 19.70% | 0.82% | 4.16% |
| h | 0.00% | 0.00% | 0.00% | #DIV/0! |
| k | 13.13% | 9.39% | 3.74% | 39.85% |
| m | 248.19% | 231.46% | 16.72% | 7.22% |
| n | 3.30% | 3.36% | -0.06% | -1.79% |
| o | 13.95% | 13.43% | 0.52% | 3.91% |
| r | 8.20% | 7.79% | 0.41% | 5.31% |
| u | 25.83% | 24.54% | 1.29% | 5.24% |
| w | (10.12) | (9.52) | (0.61) | 6.37% |
| x | 56.44% | 59.12% | -2.69% | -4.55% |
| z | 27.04% | 28.45% | -1.40% | -4.93% |

It still has the superior sales or revenue voulume (**S**), which is even more than double of its wealth or total assets (**W**). Their hypermarket is an excellent cash generator that always brings money to move it on.

Its problem now is just managing its **X** and iits **Z**, which already better, since both of them already lower than its 2008. Sure that its management had known that those two items must pushed lower, but without clear blue print.

# CHAPTER-VII: The *Beaux Arts*[131] in Finance

The wealth or total assets (**W**) divided to current assets ( **C**) and non current assets (**N**) or **W**=(**C**+**N**).

| C | W |
|---|---|
| N | |

The **C** itself consist of kind of cash (**K**), job account receivables (**J**) and procured inventory (**P**) or **C**=(**K**+**J**+**P**).

| K | C |
|---|---|
| J | |
| P | |

Normally the total of K and J already equal or greater than the xpress debt (**X**) or (**K**+**J**) =>**X**.

| K | X |
|---|---|
| J | |

So then, since **C**=(**K**+**J**+**P**) so **C** is greater than **X** or **C**>**X**, because (**K**+**J**+**P**) > (**K**+**J**), if **K**>0, **J**>0 and **P**>0.

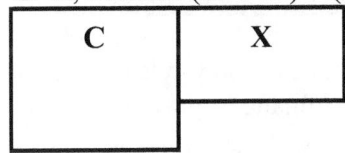

Since **W** is the total of equity (**E**) and liabilities (**L**), **L** is less or equal than **E** so **W**=(**E**+**L**) or **W** is less than **2E**.

| W | L |
|---|---|
| | E |

# Carefour's Accounting *Newtonian Gravity*[132]

Let's say that the management of Carefour facing similar but bigger problem than Wal-Mart.

|   | 2010 | 2009 | (+) | (%) |
|---|---|---|---|---|
| c | 125.00% | 32.71% | 92.29% | 282.19% |
| d | 30.00% | 28.45% | 1.55% | 5.46% |
| f | 15.00% | 20.02% | -5.02% | -25.09% |
| g | 75.00 | 86.89 | (11.89) | -13.68% |
| i | 2.00% | 0.00% | 2.00% | #DIV/0! |
| j | 6.00 | 9.23 | (3.23) | -35.00% |
| l | 200.00% | 363.81% | -163.81% | -45.03% |
| p | 30.00 | 35.26 | (5.26) | -14.92% |
| q | 100.00% | 14.84% | 85.16% | 573.93% |
| s | 10.00% | -1.09% | 11.09% | -1019.16% |
| t | 30.00% | 73.20% | -43.20% | -59.01% |
| v | 75.00% | 78.02% | -3.02% | -3.87% |
| y | 30.00% | 0.00% | 30.00% | #DIV/0! |

Then they want to have better 13 key-piles ratios for 2010 based opn the 2009 finance gravity. Major improvement needed for **c**, **f**, **j**, **l**, **p**, **q**, **s** key-piles. Moderate improvement done for **d** and **y** *key-piles*. Just harmonic targets set for **g**, **i**, **t**, **v** *key-piles* ratios. In finance architecture, all 13 (thirteen) sensitifity analysis be done.

This is extremely valid for 13 *key-piles* ratio, but will not be applicable for remaining *locked-stones* ratios.

## Relativistic Mechanics[133] in Carefour Finance

Desired sales or revenue (**S**) is previous sales or revenue (**S'**), grown by sales grow $s=(S/S')-1$ or $S=(1+s)S'$.

| 96,007 | 72,005 | | | | |
|---|---|---|---|---|---|
| latest | 24,002 | 14,401 | | | |
| | 9,601 | 1,920 | | | |
| | | 7,681 | 2,304 | | |
| | | | 5,376 | 1,613 | 484 |
| previous | | | | | 1,129 |
| 87,279 | | | | 3,763 | |

**Carefour-10**

| 22,402 | 30,002 | 44,635 | 29,757 | 24,002 | 15,001 |
|---|---|---|---|---|---|
| 1,600 | | | | | 9,001 |
| 6,000 | | | | 5,755 | |
| | 14,633 | | 14,878 | 11,115 | |
| | | | | 3,763 | |

Its variable or cost of goods (**V**) following the desired variable portion $(v)=(V/S)$, so then $V=(Sv)=(1+s)S'v$. So, the marginal contribution $M=(S-V)=(1-v)S=(1-v)(1+s)S'$. Its fixed cost (**F**) will follow the fixed cost portion is $(f=F/S)$, so $F=(Sf)=(1+s)S'f$. Its operational surplus $(O)=(M-F)=(1-v)S-Sf=(1-v-f)S=(1-v-f)(1+s)S'$.

If investment or financial cost (**I**) following as portion of its ratio $(i)=(I/S)$, then $(I)=(Si)=(1+s)S'i$. Before tax income $(B)=(O-I)=(M-F-I)=(S-V-F-I)=S-Sv-Sf-Si=S(1-v-f-i)=(1-v-f-i)(1+s)S'$ as Paccioli[134] finance's law.

# Carefour 's *Photo-electrics*[135] in Accountancy

As the financial energies flown from page **1-85** above, its next accounting consequences will looks easier.

|   | 2010 | 2009 | (+) | (%) |
|---|------|------|-----|-----|
| a | 12.05% | 0.89% | 11.16% | 1258.78% |
| b | 17.21% | 3.31% | 13.90% | 420.29% |
| e | 25.29% | 2.94% | 22.35% | 759.79% |
| h | 10.16% | 0.00% | 10.16% | #DIV/0! |
| k | 93.33% | 8.84% | 84.49% | 955.45% |
| m | 215.09% | 169.30% | 45.79% | 27.05% |
| n | 3.92% | 0.37% | 3.55% | 946.28% |
| o | 21.51% | 3.31% | 18.20% | 550.36% |
| r | 8.43% | 0.63% | 7.80% | 1229.28% |
| u | 33.86% | 3.03% | 30.83% | 1017.05% |
| w | 39.00 | 42.40 | (3.40) | -8.01% |
| x | 80.66% | 92.31% | -11.65% | -12.62% |
| z | 30.25% | 51.67% | -21.42% | -41.46% |

After tax (**A**) is before tax (**B**) less tax (**T**) or **A**=(**B**-**T**), on the tax rate (**t**) as portion of **B**, as **t**= (**T**/**B**) or **T**= (**Bt**), so **A**=(**B**-**T**)=(**B**-**Bt**)=**B**(1-**t**)= (**S**-**V**-**F**-**I**)(1-**t**)= **S**(1-**t**)(1-**v**-**f**-**i**)=(1+**s**)(1-**t**)(1+**v**+**f**+**i**)**S**'. So then, retained earnings (**E**)=after tax(**A**) less dividend(**D**) or **R**=(**A**-**D**), on dividend payout (**d**) as portion of **A**, as **d**=(**D**/**A**) or **D**=(**Ad**), so then **R**=(**A**-**D**)=(**A**-**Ad**)=**A**(1-**d**)=(1-**d**)(**S**-**V**-**F**-**I**)(1-**t**)= is equal to **S**(1-**d**)(1-**t**)(1-**v**-**f**-**i**)=(1-**d**)(1+**s**)(1-**t**)(1-**v**-**f**-**i**)**S**' to equity.

# *Orientation* Mandala[136] of Carefour Finance

As the financial energies flown from page **1-86** above, its next finance architecture design will be easier.

|   | 2010 | 2009 | (+) | (%) |
|---|---|---|---|---|
| A | 5,376 | 457 | 4,919 | 1076.45% |
| B | 7,681 | 1,705 | 5,976 | 350.47% |
| C | 30,002 | 12,209 | 17,793 | 145.74% |
| D | 1,613 | 130 | 1,483 | 1140.70% |
| E | 14,878 | 11,115 | 3,763 | 33.86% |
| F | 14,401 | 17,476 | (3,075) | -17.60% |
| G | 15,001 | 16,436 | (1,435) | -8.73% |
| H | 1,129 | - | 1,129 | #DIV/0! |
| I | 1,920 | - | 1,920 | #DIV/0! |
| J | 6,000 | 2,238 | 3,762 | 168.12% |
| K | 1,600 | 3,301 | (1,701) | -51.53% |
| L | 29,757 | 40,438 | (10,681) | -26.41% |
| M | 24,002 | 19,181 | 4,821 | 25.13% |

The home taken or net dividend (**H**)= dividend (**D**) less yielding tax of dividend (**y**) or **H=(D-Y)**, on yielding tax of dividend (**y**) as portion of **D**, as **y=(Y/D)** or **Y=(Dy)**, so then **H=(D-Y)=(D-Dy)=D(1-y)=Ad(1-y)=d(1-y)(S-V-F-I)(1-t)=Sd(1-y)(1-t)(1-v-f-i)=(1-y)(1+s)(1-t)(1-v-f-i)S'd**.

Please do not be confuse, (with its long algebraic expression), that all accountants already familiar with those Paccioli's law, and for the architects? *Look at its boxes!*

As the financial energies flown from page **1-87** above, its next balance-sheet architecture, will be easier.

|   | 2010 | 2009 | (+) | (%) |
|---|------|------|-----|-----|
| N | 14,633 | 39,344 | (24,711) | -62.81% |
| O | 9,601 | 1,705 | 7,896 | 463.09% |
| P | 6,000 | 6,670 | (670) | -10.04% |
| Q | 5,755 | 3,109 | 2,646 | 85.11% |
| R | 3,763 | 327 | 3,436 | 1050.91% |
| S | 96,007 | 87,279 | 8,728 | 10.00% |
| T | 2,304 | 1,248 | 1,056 | 84.63% |
| U | 11,115 | 10,788 | 327 | 3.03% |
| V | 72,005 | 68,098 | 3,907 | 5.74% |
| W | 44,635 | 51,553 | (6,918) | -13.42% |
| X | 24,002 | 37,329 | (13,327) | -35.70% |
| Y | 484 | - | 484 | #DIV/0! |
| Z | 9,001 | 20,893 | (11,892) | -56.92% |

Retained earnings (**E**)=after tax(**A**) less dividend(**D**) or **R**=(**A-D**), on dividend payout (**d**) as portion of **A**, as **d**=(**D/A**) or **D**=(**Ad**), so then **R**=(**A-D**)= (**A-Ad**)= **A**(1-**d**)= (1-**d**)(**S-V-F-I**)(1-**t**)= **S**(1-**d**)(1-**t**)(1-**v-f-i**)= (1-**d**)(1+**s**)(1-**t**) (1-**v-f-i**)**S'** then added to its utilized equity (**U**), or previous equity (**E'**) to construct a new equity position (**E**)=(**E'+R**)= **U**+(**A-D**)=**U**+(**A-Ad**)=**U**+**A**(1-**d**)=**U**+(1-**d**)(**S-V-F-I**)(1-**t**)= **U**+**S**(1-**d**)(1-**t**) (1-**v-f-i**)= **U**+(1-**d**)(1+**s**)(1-**t**)(1-**v-f-i**)**S'**.

As the financial energies flown from page **1-88** above, its next balance-sheet architecture, will be easier.

| 87,279 | 68,098 | | | | | |
|---|---|---|---|---|---|---|
| latest | 19,181 | 17,476 | | | | |
| | | 1,705 | - | | | |
| | | | 1,705 | 1,248 | | |
| | | | | 457 | 130 | - |
| | | | | | | - |
| previous | | | | | 327 | |
| 88,239 | | | | | | |

**Carefour-09**

| 3,301 | 12,209 | 51,553 | 40,438 | 37,329 | 16,436 |
|---|---|---|---|---|---|
| 2,238 | | | | | 20,893 |
| 6,670 | | | | 3,109 | |
| | 39,344 | | 11,115 | 10,788 | |
| | | | | 327 | |

Understanding that leverage or gearing ratio $(l)$= $(L/E)$ then its liability $(L)=El=l(E'+R)=l\{U+(A-D)\}=l\{U+(A-Ad)\}=l\{U+A(1-d)\}=l\{U+(1-d)(S-V-F-I)(1-t)\}=l\{U+S(1-d)(1-t)(1-v-f-i)\}=l\{U+(1-d)(1+s)(1-t)(1-v-f-i)S'\}$.

Because wealth or total assets $(W)=(L+E)$ so $W=$ $(E+El)=E(1+l)(E'+R)=(1+l)\{U+(A-D)\}=(1+l)\{U+(A-Ad)=(1+l)\{U+A(1-d)\}=(1+l)\{U+(1-d)(S-V-F-I)(1-t)\}=(1+l)\{U+S(1-d)(1-t)(1-v-f-i)\}=S'(1+l)\{U+(1-d)(1+s)(1-t)(1-v-f-i)\}$. Please remember that its procurred inventory $(p)=$ $360P/V$ so $P=Vp/360=Svp/360=S'(1+s)(vp/360)$.

As the financial energies flown from page **1-89** above, its next balance-sheet architecture, will be easier.

| 88,239 | 68,719 | | | | | |
|---|---|---|---|---|---|---|
| latest | 19,520 | 16,791 | | | | |
| | | 2,729 | - | | | |
| | | | 2,729 | 1,241 | | |
| | | | | 1,488 | 219 | - |
| previous | | | | | | - |
| - | | | | | 1,269 | |

**Carefour-08**

| 5,317 | 15,364 | 52,288 | 41,365 | 38,597 | 17,211 |
|---|---|---|---|---|---|
| 3,156 | | | | | 21,386 |
| 6,891 | | | | 2,768 | |
| | 36,924 | | 10,923 | 9,654 | |
| | | | | 1,269 | |

Please consider that current ratio (**c**) is the fraction of current assets (**C**) compared to its xpress liabilities (**X**) while **C** is the total of its kind of cash (**K**), job account receivables (**J**) and procured inventory (**P**). Its current ratio **c**=(**C/X**)= (**K+J+P**)/**X** or **C=Xc**, while its quick or acid test ratio (**q**)=(**C-P**)/**X** or (**C-P**)=**Xq** or **C**=(**Xq+P**).

Combining the two, since (**C=C**), then (**Xq+P**)=**Xc** or **P**=(**Xc-Xq**) or **P=X(c-q)**, so then **X=P/(c-q)** known. Since procured inventory days (**p**)=360**P**/**V** so **P=Vp/360**= **Svp/360=S'(1+s)(vp/360)** and **X=S'(1+s)(vp/360)/(c-q)**.

# Financial *Electro-magnetic Duality*[140] of Carefour

As the financial energies flown from page **1-90** above, its next balance-sheet architecture, will be easier.

|   | 2009 | 2008 | (+) | (%) |
|---|------|------|-----|-----|
| c | 32.71% | 39.81% | -7.10% | -17.84% |
| d | 28.45% | 14.72% | 13.73% | 93.28% |
| f | 20.02% | 19.03% | 0.99% | 5.22% |
| g | 86.89 | 90.16 | (3.27) | -3.63% |
| i | 0.00% | 0.00% | 0.00% | #DIV/0! |
| j | 9.23 | 12.88 | (3.64) | -28.31% |
| l | 363.81% | 378.70% | -14.88% | -3.93% |
| p | 35.26 | 36.10 | (0.84) | -2.32% |
| q | 14.84% | 21.95% | -7.11% | -32.41% |
| s | -1.09% | | | |
| t | 73.20% | 45.47% | 27.72% | 60.96% |
| v | 78.02% | 77.88% | 0.15% | 0.19% |
| y | 0.00% | 0.00% | 0.00% | #DIV/0! |

Since **W**, **E**, **L** and **X** known then its quoted long-term debt $(\mathbf{Q})=(\mathbf{L\text{-}X})=\mathbf{El\text{-}P}/(\mathbf{c\text{-}q})=\mathbf{l(E'+R)}-(\mathbf{Vp}/360)/(\mathbf{c\text{-}q})= \mathbf{l\{U+(A\text{-}D)\}}-(\mathbf{Svp}/360)/(\mathbf{c\text{-}q})=\mathbf{l\{U+(A\text{-}Ad)}-(\mathbf{Svp}/360)/(\mathbf{c\text{-}q}) =\mathbf{l\{U+A(1\text{-}d)\}}-(\mathbf{Svp}/360)/(\mathbf{c\text{-}q})=\mathbf{l\{U+(1\text{-}d)(S\text{-}V\text{-}F\text{-}I)(1\text{-}t)\}}- (\mathbf{Svp}/360)/(\mathbf{c\text{-}q})=\mathbf{l\{U+S(1\text{-}d)(1\text{-}t)(1\text{-}v\text{-}f\text{-}i)\}}-(\mathbf{Svp}/360)/(\mathbf{c\text{-}q}) = \mathbf{l\{U+S(1\text{-}d)\ (1\text{-}t)(1\text{-}v\text{-}f\text{-}i)\}}-(\mathbf{Svp}/360)/(\mathbf{c\text{-}q}) = \mathbf{Ul+Sl(1\text{-}d)} (1\text{-}t)(1\text{-}v\text{-}f\text{-}i)\}}-(\mathbf{Svp}/360)/(\mathbf{c\text{-}q})=\mathbf{Ul+S\{l(1\text{-}d)(1\text{-}t)(1\text{-}v\text{-}f\text{-}i)\}}- (\mathbf{vp}/360)/(\mathbf{c\text{-}q})\}$. Now its quoted long-term debt (**Q**) known.

As the financial energies flown from page **1-91** above, its next balance-sheet architecture, will be easier.

|   | 2009 | 2008 | (+) | (%) |
|---|---|---|---|---|
| a | 0.89% | 2.85% | -1.96% | -68.85% |
| b | 3.31% | 5.22% | -1.91% | -36.63% |
| e | 2.94% | 11.62% | -8.68% | -74.68% |
| h | 0.00% | 0.00% | 0.00% | #DIV/0! |
| k | 8.84% | 13.78% | -4.93% | -35.81% |
| m | 169.30% | 168.76% | 0.54% | 0.32% |
| n | 0.37% | 1.44% | -1.06% | -73.95% |
| o | 3.31% | 5.22% | -1.91% | -36.63% |
| r | 0.63% | 2.43% | -1.79% | -73.86% |
| u | 3.03% | 13.14% | -10.11% | -76.94% |
| w | 42.40 | 41.19 | 1.21 | 2.94% |
| x | 92.31% | 93.31% | -1.00% | -1.07% |
| z | 51.67% | 51.70% | -0.03% | -0.07% |

On its liability side, goods trade account payable (**G**) related to its goods payable days (**g**)=360**G**/**V**) or **G**=(**Vg**/360)=(**Svg**/360)=(1+**s**)(**S'vg**/360).

Its zero trade xpress debt (**Z**)=(**X-G**)={**P**/(**c-q**)}-**G**= (**Vp**/360)/(**c-q**)-(**Vg**/360)=(**V**/360){**p**/(**c-q**)-**g**} =(**Sv**/360) {**p**/(**c-q**)-**g**}=(1+**s**)(**S'v**/360){**p**/(**c-q**)-**g**}.

Now, we know the **A** to **Z** alphabeth abbreviations, all of our finance architecture jargon, except **J**, **K** and **N**.

# Financial *Durabilities*[142] and Carefour

As the financial energies flown from page **1-92** above, its next balance-sheet architecture, will be easier.

|   | 2009 | 2008 | (+) | (%) |
|---|------|------|-----|-----|
| A | 457 | 1,488 | (1,031) | -69.29% |
| B | 1,705 | 2,729 | (1,024) | -37.52% |
| C | 12,209 | 15,364 | (3,155) | -20.54% |
| D | 130.00 | 219.00 | (89) | -40.64% |
| E | 11,115 | 10,923 | 192 | 1.76% |
| F | 17,476 | 16,791 | 685 | 4.08% |
| G | 16,436 | 17,211 | (775) | -4.50% |
| H | - | - | - | #DIV/0! |
| I | - | - | - | #DIV/0! |
| J | 2,238 | 3,156 | (918) | -29.09% |
| K | 3,301 | 5,317 | (2,016) | -37.92% |
| L | 40,438 | 41,365 | (927) | -2.24% |
| M | 19,181 | 19,520 | (339) | -1.74% |

On its asset side, its job or trade account receivable (**J**) related to its job or trade account receivable days (**j**)=360**J**/**S**) or **J**=(**Sj**/360) =(1+**s**)(**S'j**/360).

Its kind of cash (**K**)=**C**-(**J-P**)=**Xc**-(**Si**/360)-(**Vp**/360) =**Pc**/(**c-q**)-(**Sj**/360)-**S**(**vp**/360)  =**Vpc**/{360(**c-q**)}-(**Sj**/360)-**S**(**vp**/360)  =**Svpc**/{360(**c-q**)}-(**Sj**/360)-**S**(**vp**/360)= (**S**/360) {(**vpc**)/(**c-q**)-**j**-**vp**}=(**S**/360)[**vp**{**c**/(**c-q**)-1}-**j**]=(1+**s**)(**S'**/360) [**vp**{**c**/(**c-q**)}-1}-**j**]. Just item (N) had not been computed.

## *Less is More* **Principle in  Carefour**

As the financial energies flown from page 1-**93** above, its next balance-sheet architecture, will be easier.

|   | 2009 | 2008 | (+) | (%) |
|---|------|------|-----|-----|
| N | 39,344 | 36,924 | 2,420 | 6.55% |
| O | 1,705 | 2,729 | (1,024) | -37.52% |
| P | 6,670 | 6,891 | (221) | -3.21% |
| Q | 3,109 | 2,768 | 341 | 12.32% |
| R | 327 | 1,269 | (942) | -74.23% |
| S | 87,279 | 88,239 | (960) | -1.09% |
| T | 1,248 | 1,241.00 | 7 | 0.56% |
| U | 10,788 | 9,654 | 1,134 | 11.75% |
| V | 68,098 | 68,719 | (621) | -0.90% |
| W | 51,553 | 52,288 | (735) | -1.41% |
| X | 37,329 | 38,597 | (1,268) | -3.29% |
| Y | - | - | - | #DIV/0! |
| Z | 20,893 | 21,386 | (493) | -2.31% |

Finally its non current assets $(N)=(W-C)$
$=(El-Xc)=l(U+R)-Pc/(c-q)\}=l(U+R)-Vpc/\{360(c-q)\}$
$=l(U+R)-Svpc/\{360(c-q)\}=l\{U+S(1-d)(1-t)(1-v-f-i)\}-$
$Svpc/\{360(c-q)\}=Ul+S[l(1-d)(1-t)(1-v-f-i)-vpc/\{360(c-q)\}$

Carefour management and its finance consultants, now can enjoy the suggested radical but extremely realistic financial improvement quickly. They can choose finance *architecture* or finance *algebra* as well, but *not* T-account.

Boeing's case leads to the discussion on the role of equity (**E**) and non current assets (**N**) management.

| N | E |
|---|---|
|   |   |

In normal condition the **E** must be greater or equal than its **N** or (**E** => **N**). Since **E** consist of retained earnings (**R** ) and utilized equity at the beginning (**U**), then

| E | U |
|---|---|
|   | R |

It will be better if **N**, is less or equal to **U** or simply (**N** <=**U**). Since **R** will only exist at the end of its operation.

| N | U |
|---|---|
|   | R |

In more complex condition, if (**N** > **E**), then it must be financed by quoted long-term debt (**Q**), but (**Q+E**) > **N**.

| C | X |
|---|---|
|   | Q |
| N |   |
|   | E |

So then some of the **Q**. could be used to providing current assets ( **C**), since **C** must be greater than the total of xpress debts (**X**), or (**C** >**X**).

# _Post Modern_[144] **Accountancy Architecture for Boeing**

Please look at visuals af pages **95-106**, to show you how we build finance architecture construction of Boeing. We can also apply these ideas to any other **_IFRS_** formats.

|   | 2010 | 2009 | (+) | (%) |
|---|---|---|---|---|
| c | 130.00% | 97.11% | 32.89% | 33.87% |
| d | 20.00% | 1.72% | 18.28% | 1060.87% |
| f | 10.00% | 14.16% | -4.16% | -29.40% |
| g | 180.00 | 45.18 | 134.82 | 298.39% |
| i | 2.00% | 0.50% | 1.50% | 302.84% |
| j | 30.00 | 30.50 | (0.50) | -1.64% |
| l | 2500.00% | 2688.90% | -188.90% | -7.03% |
| p | 90.00 | 107.82 | (17.82) | -16.52% |
| q | 100.00% | 45.62% | 54.38% | 119.22% |
| s | 20.00% | 12.10% | 7.90% | 65.24% |
| t | 30.00% | 22.88% | 7.12% | 31.14% |
| v | 80.00% | 82.80% | -2.80% | -3.39% |
| y | 30.00% | 0.00% | 30.00% | #DIV/0! |

By the end of 2010 Boeing can have 20% sales or revenue growth (**s**). We know that its previous sales or revenue (**S'**)= 68,281 or growing (**s'**)= 12.10% from its two years ago **S"**=60,909. So it is realistic and no big deal, **S**=(1+**s**)**S'** =(1+20%) x 68,281= 81,937. _It is so easy!_

Then we follow the key-piles and lock-stone ratios to complete all it's **A** to **Z** finance items and **a** to **z** ratios.

If it needs variable portion (**v**)=80%, its variable xpenses (**V**)=**Sv**=81,937x80%= 65,550. So then its margin of contribution (**M**)= (**S-V**)= 81,937-65,550= 16,387.

| 81,937 | 65,550 | | | | | |
|---|---|---|---|---|---|---|
| latest | 16,387 | 8,194 | | | | |
| | | 8,194 | 1,639 | | | |
| | | | 6,555 | 1,966 | | |
| | | | | 4,588 | 918 | 275 |
| previous | | | | | | 642 |
| 68,281 | | | | | 3,671 | |

**BA-Boeing-10**

| 47,797 | 71,012 | 153,290 | 147,395 | 54,625 | 32,775 |
|---|---|---|---|---|---|
| 6,828 | | | | | 21,850 |
| 16,387 | | | | 92,770 | |
| | 82,278 | | 5,896 | 2,225 | |
| | | | | 3,671 | |

If it needs fixed portion (**f**)=10%, its fixed xpenses (**F**)=**Sf**=81,937x10%= 8,194. So then its operational surplus (**O**)= (**M-F**)= 16,387-8,194= 8,194.

If it also needs investment or financial portion (**i**)=2%, its investment or financial xpenses (**I**)=**Si**= 81,937x2%= 1,639. So then its before tax income (**B**)= (**O-I**)= 8,194-1,639= 6,555. Looks familiar? *It's Paccioli's.*

We just translating it the visual finance architecture, geometric and algebra form, to make it better understood.

# Accounting *Rhythm*[148] and *Contrast*[149] of Boeing

If it needs tax rate (**t**)=30%, its tax paid (**T**)= **Bt**=6,555x30%= 1,966. So then its after tax income (**A**)= (**B-T**)= 6,555-1,966= 4,588.

|   | 2010 | 2009 | (+) | (%) |
|---|------|------|-----|-----|
| a | 2.99% | 2.15% | 0.84% | 39.13% |
| b | 4.28% | 2.79% | 1.49% | 53.29% |
| e | 62.26% | 58.97% | 3.29% | 5.59% |
| h | 28.87% | 0.00% | 28.87% | #DIV/0! |
| k | 87.50% | 28.02% | 59.48% | 212.24% |
| m | 53.45% | 110.04% | -56.58% | -51.42% |
| n | 4.48% | 1.92% | 2.56% | 133.15% |
| o | 5.35% | 3.34% | 2.01% | 60.24% |
| r | 2.39% | 2.11% | 0.28% | 13.26% |
| u | 164.98% | 143.70% | 21.28% | 14.81% |
| w | 60.00 | (93.13) | 153.13 | -164.42% |
| x | 37.06% | 54.96% | -17.90% | -32.57% |
| z | 14.82% | 43.10% | -28.28% | -65.61% |

If it also needs dividend payout rate (**d**)=20%, its dividend paid (**D**)=**Ad**= 4,588x20%= 918. So then its retained earnings (**R**)= (**A-D**)= 4,588-918= 3,671.

If it also needs yielding tax of dividend (**y**)=30%, its yielding tax paid (**Y**)=**Dy**= 918x30%= 275. So then its home taken dividend (**H**)= (**D-Y**)= 918-275= 642.

They are very simple for Income Statement items.

Now, let's try its Balanche-sheet items. Its utilized capital at the beginning (**U**) is the equity at the end of the previous year (**E'**), so then (**U=E'**), then **E**=(**U+R**)=2,225 +3,671=5,896. It's also still following *Paccioli's rule*.

|   | 2010 | 2009 | (+) | (%) |
|---|---|---|---|---|
| A | 4,588 | 1,335 | 3,253 | 243.71% |
| B | 6,555 | 1,731 | 4,824 | 278.68% |
| C | 71,012 | 31,933 | 39,079 | 122.38% |
| D | 918 | 23 | 895 | 3889.99% |
| E | 5,896 | 2,225 | 3,671 | 164.98% |
| F | 8,194 | 9,671 | (1,477) | -15.28% |
| G | 32,775 | 7,096 | 25,679 | 361.88% |
| H | 642 | - | 642 | #DIV/0! |
| I | 1,639 | 339 | 1,300 | 383.41% |
| J | 16,387 | 5,785 | 10,602 | 183.27% |
| K | 6,828 | 9,215 | (2,387) | -25.90% |
| L | 147,395 | 59,828 | 87,567 | 146.36% |
| M | 16,387 | 11,741 | 4,646 | 39.57% |

If it in the urgency needs leverage or gearing ratio (**l**)=2,500%, its liability at the total (**L**)=**El**= 5,896x2500%= 147,395. So then its wealth or total asset (**W**)=(**E+L**)= 5,896+147,395= 153,290.

If it needs the procured inventory days (**p**)=90, its procured inventory (**P**)=(**Vp**/360)=65,550x90/360= 16,387.

# *Forces* of Static[151] Accounting Mechanics of Boeing

Let's deal with the current ratio $(c)=(C/X)=130\%$ and quick or acid test ratio $(q)=(C-P)/X=100\%$ concepts.

|   | 2010 | 2009 | (+) | (%) |
|---|---|---|---|---|
| N | 82,278 | 30,120 | 52,158 | 173.17% |
| O | 8,194 | 2,070 | 6,124 | 295.83% |
| P | 16,387 | 16,933 | (546) | -3.22% |
| Q | 92,770 | 26,945 | 65,825 | 244.29% |
| R | 3,671 | 1,312 | 2,359 | 179.79% |
| S | 81,937 | 68,281 | 13,656 | 20.00% |
| T | 1,966 | 396 | 1,570 | 396.59% |
| U | 2,225 | 913 | 1,312 | 143.70% |
| V | 65,550 | 56,540 | 9,010 | 15.94% |
| W | 153,290 | 62,053 | 91,237 | 147.03% |
| X | 54,625 | 32,883 | 21,742 | 66.12% |
| Y | 275 | - | 275 | #DIV/0! |
| Z | 21,850 | 25,787 | (3,937) | -15.27% |

Since $c=(C/X)$ then $C=Xc$ and since $q=(C-P)/X$, then $(C-P)=Xq$ or $C=Xq+P$. It means that $(C=C)$ or $Xc=Xq+P$, so $(Xc-Xq)=P$ or $X(c-q)=P$, then $X=P/(c-q)=$ 16,387 /(130%-100%)=(16,387/30%)=54,625.

So, $C=Xc=$ 54,625 x 130%=71,012 and the quoted long-term debt $(Q)=(L-X)=147,395-54,625=92,770$. If it needs good or trade account payable days $(g)=180$, its good payable $(G)=(Vg/360)=65,550x180/360= 32,775$.

# Boeing Accounting and *Maxwell's* Field[152] Concern

So then its zero trade related xpress debt that must be paid quickly (**Z**)= (**X-G**)= 54,625-32,775= 21,850.

| 68,281 | 56,540 | | | | | |
|--------|--------|-------|------|-------|-----|---|
| latest | 11,741 | 9,671 | | | | |
| | | 2,070 | 339 | | | |
| | | | 1,731 | 396 | | |
| | | | | 1,335 | 23 | - |
| previous | | | | | | - |
| 60,909 | | | | | 1,312 | |

**BA-Boeing-09**

| 9,215 | 31,933 | 62,053 | 59,828 | 32,883 | 7,096 |
|-------|--------|--------|--------|--------|-------|
| 5,785 | | | | | 25,787 |
| 16,933 | | | | 26,945 | |
| | 30,120 | | 2,225 | 913 | |
| | | | | 1,312 | |

If it also needs job trade account receivable days (**j**)=30, its job trade account receivables (**J**)=(**Sj**/360)= 81,937x30/360=6,828. So then its kind of cash (**K**)= (**C-J-P**)= 71,012-6,828-16,387= 47,797. *Boeing needs it as big.*

So then its total non current, fix and intangible assets (**N**)= (**W-C**)= 153,290-71,012= 82,278.

Mission accomplished, the finance algebra has identified all **A** to **Z** financial architecture items, coherence with *IFRS* standards, and finance architecture made easy. Is it easier? Please ask all world leading *finance professors*!

# Accounting *Scale*[153] and Accentuation[154] of Boeing

Do we need to analyze this suggested Boeing finance architecture blue-print? Not necessary, but we do!

| | | | | | | |
|---|---|---|---|---|---|---|
| 60,909 | 50,352 | | | | | |
| latest | 10,557 | 6,360 | | | | |
| | | 4,197 | 202 | | | |
| | | | 3,995 | 1,341 | | |
| | | | | 2,654 | (18) | - |
| previous | | | | | | - |
| - | | | | | 2,672 | |

**BA-Boeing-08**

| | | | | | |
|---|---|---|---|---|---|
| 3,268 | 24,482 | 53,779 | 54,921 | 30,773 | 5,871 |
| 5,602 | | | | | 24,902 |
| 15,612 | | | | 24,148 | |
| | 29,297 | | (1,142) | (3,814) | |
| | | | | 2,672 | |

The-26 **IFRS'** (*International Finance Reporting Standard*'s) ratios consist of 13 financial architecture key-piles[33] and 13 others locked-stones[34]. The-13 key-piles are:

01: **c**= Current ratio= (**C/X**)=71,012/54,625=**130.00%**

02: **d**= Dividend paid portion to after tax= (**D/A**)= 918/4,588= **20.00%**, *it's sharp!!*

03: **f**= Fix expenses portion to revenue= (**F/S**)= 8,194/81,937= **10.00%**, *it's sharp!!*

04: **g**= Goods or trade account payable days= (360**G/V**)= 360x32,775/65,550= **180.00**, *it's sharp!!*

05: $i$= Investment or financial portion to revenue= $(I/S)$=
   1,639/81,937=**2.00%**, *it's sharp!!*
06: $j$= Job or trade account receivable days= $(360J/S)$=
   360x6,828/81,937=**30.00**, *it's sharp!!*

|   | 2009 | 2008 | (+) | (%) |
|---|---|---|---|---|
| A | 1,335 | 2,654 | (1,319) | -49.70% |
| B | 1,731 | 3,995 | (2,264) | -56.67% |
| C | 31,933 | 24,482 | 7,451 | 30.43% |
| D | 23.00 | (18.00) | 41 | -227.78% |
| E | 2,225 | (1,142) | 3,367 | -294.83% |
| F | 9,671 | 6,360 | 3,311 | 52.06% |
| G | 7,096 | 5,871 | 1,225 | 20.87% |
| H | - | - | - | #DIV/0! |
| I | 339 | 202 | 137 | 67.82% |
| J | 5,785 | 5,602 | 183 | 3.27% |
| K | 9,215 | 3,268 | 5,947 | 181.98% |
| L | 59,828 | 54,921 | 4,907 | 8.93% |
| M | 11,741 | 10,557 | 1,184 | 11.22% |

07: $l$= Leverage or gearing = debt equity ratio= *DER*=
   $(L/E)$=147,395/5,896=**2,500.00%**, *it's sharp!!*
08: $p$= Procurred inventory days= $(360P/V)$=360x16,387
   /65,550=**90.00**, *it's sharp!!*
09: $q$= Quick or acid test ratio= $(C-P)/X$=(71,012-16,387)
   /54,625=**100.00%**, *it's sharp!!*

# Financial *Drainage*[156] and *Sanitary*[157] for Boeing

10: **s**= Sales or revenue growth to previous= $(S/S'-1)$=
   81,937/68,281-1=**20.00%**, *it's sharp!!*

|   | 2009 | 2008 | (+) | (%) |
|---|------|------|-----|-----|
| N | 30,120 | 29,297 | 823 | 2.81% |
| O | 2,070 | 4,197 | (2,127) | -50.68% |
| P | 16,933 | 15,612 | 1,321 | 8.46% |
| Q | 26,945 | 24,148 | 2,797 | 11.58% |
| R | 1,312 | 2,672 | (1,360) | -50.90% |
| S | 68,281 | 60,909 | 7,372 | 12.10% |
| T | 396 | 1,341.00 | (945) | -70.47% |
| U | 913 | (3,814) | 4,727 | -123.94% |
| V | 56,540 | 50,352 | 6,188 | 12.29% |
| W | 62,053 | 53,779 | 8,274 | 15.39% |
| X | 32,883 | 30,773 | 2,110 | 6.86% |
| Y | - | - | - | #DIV/0! |
| Z | 25,787 | 24,902 | 885 | 3.55% |

11: **t**= Tax rate or portion to before tax earnings= $(T/B)$=
   1,966/6,555=**30.00%**, *it's sharp!!*
12: **v**= Variable expenses portion to revenue= $(V/S)$=
   65,550/81,937=**80.00%**, *it's sharp!!*
13: **y**= Yielding tax of the dividend paid= $(Y/D)$= 275/918=
   **30.00%**, *it's sharp!!*
   All 13 (thirteen) *key-pile* finance architecture ratios
can be set sharp, and guaranteed to perform accurately sharp

# Boeing The *Path*[158] and *Nodes* of Accountancy

The 13 (thirteen) *locked-stone* finance architecture ratios just a derivative of its *key-piles* ratio and not sharp.

|   | 2009 | 2008 | (+) | (%) |
|---|------|------|-----|-----|
| c | 97.11% | 79.56% | 17.55% | 22.07% |
| d | 1.72% | -0.68% | 2.40% | -354.02% |
| f | 14.16% | 10.44% | 3.72% | 35.64% |
| g | 45.18 | 41.98 | 3.21 | 7.64% |
| i | 0.50% | 0.33% | 0.16% | 49.70% |
| j | 30.50 | 33.11 | (2.61) | -7.88% |
| l | 2688.90% | -4809.19% | 7498.09% | -155.91% |
| p | 107.82 | 111.62 | (3.81) | -3.41% |
| q | 45.62% | 28.82% | 16.79% | 58.26% |
| s | 12.10% |  |  |  |
| t | 22.88% | 33.57% | -10.69% | -31.85% |
| v | 82.80% | 82.67% | 0.14% | 0.17% |
| y | 0.00% | 0.00% | 0.00% | #DIV/0! |

01: **a**= After tax return on asset= (**A/W**)= 4,558/153,290=**2.99%**

02: **b**= Before tax return on asset= (**B/W**)= 6,555/153,290=**4.28%**

03: **e**= Equity return= return on equity= *ROE*= (**R/E**)= 3,671/5,896=**62.26%**

04: **h**= Home taken dividend to utilized equity= (**H/U**)= 642/2,225=**28.87%**

# Financial *Oblique Access*[159] for Boeing Architecture

05. **k**= Kind of cash liquidity ratio= **(K/X)**= 47,797 /54,625=**87.50%**

|   | 2009 | 2008 | (+) | (%) |
|---|------|------|-----|-----|
| a | 2.15% | 4.94% | -2.78% | -56.41% |
| b | 2.79% | 7.43% | -4.64% | -62.45% |
| e | 58.97% | -233.98% | 292.94% | -125.20% |
| h | 0.00% | 0.00% | 0.00% | #DIV/0! |
| k | 28.02% | 10.62% | 17.40% | 163.88% |
| m | 110.04% | 113.26% | -3.22% | -2.84% |
| n | 1.92% | 4.39% | -2.47% | -56.20% |
| o | 3.34% | 7.80% | -4.47% | -57.26% |
| r | 2.11% | 4.97% | -2.85% | -57.45% |
| u | 143.70% | -70.06% | 213.76% | -305.12% |
| w | (93.13) | (102.76) | 9.62 | -9.36% |
| x | 54.96% | 56.03% | -1.07% | -1.91% |
| z | 43.10% | 45.34% | -2.24% | -4.94% |

06. **m**= Market-run or asset turn-over= *ATO*= **(S/W)**= 81,937/153,290= **53.45%**
07. **n**= NPM= net profit margin= **(R/S)**= 3,671 /81,937 =**4.48%**
08. **o**= Operational surplus to asset return= **(O/W)**= 8,194/153,290=**10.00%**
09. **r**= Return of net earnings on assets= *ROA*= **(R/W)**= 3,671/153,290=**2.39%**

The remaining 4 (four) locked-stone finance architecture ratios are as follow:

10: **u**= Utilized return on starting equity= (**R/U**)= 3,671 /2,225=**164.98%**

11: **w**= Working capital days required= (**g-p-j**)= 180.00-90.00-30.00=**60.00**, _supplier financed!_

12: **x**= Xpress or current to total debt portion= (**X/L**)= 54,625/147,395=**37.06%**

13: **z**= Zero trade liability portion of total debts= (**Z/L**)= 21,850/147,395= **14.82%**

Is it sound like some thing familiar? Yes, it's Du Pont[161] interactive financial ratio system. It is like the universal relativity, starts from Galileo[162], improved by Newton[163] and only Einstein[164] can integrate its puzzles. People saw fallen apple, only Galileo test it at Pisa tower, and Newton come with explanation, but Einstein make fundamental revisions on theory of everything.

Every body learn finance from Paccioli, but only Du Pont connecting some of the finance ratio and it stop. It is because Du Pont make 2 (two) fundamental mistakes: 1)calculating phrases against sentences not employing proper algebra notation and 2) start calculating without first standardizing (streamlining) the various financial items.

We simplify them to just 26 items of **A** to **Z** and 13 _key-pile_ finance architecture ratios, so then it can easily be calculated like Phytagorean's $X^2+Y^2=Z^2$ (pages 1-106).

Those inefficient finance algebra notations, makes it isolated and not getting ample assistance from world class mathematician for hundred of years. _It's the time now!!_

## CHAPTER-IX: 13 World-class Sacred Places

So far we have talked about1)Samsung, 2)Nestle, 3)Microsoft, 4)McDonalds, 5)Wal-Mart, 6)Carefourn and 7)Boeing. Now we'll talk about 8)British Petroleum, 9)Hyundai, 10)Daimler-Benz, 11)BMW, 12)Mitsubishi, 13)Mitsui. All selected to represent many parts of world.

| A | D |
|---|---|
|   | R |

In normal condition the dividend paid (**D**) must be less than its after tax income (**A**) or (**A** => **D**). Since **A** also consist of retained earnings (**R**)

| D | Y |
|---|---|
|   | H |

Dividend paid **D**, also subject to yielding tax of dividend (**Y**) ,before its home taken (**H**) one, or (**H**=**D**- **Y**).

| A | D | Y |
|---|---|---|
|   |   | H |
|   | R |   |

In more complex condition, if (**A** > **D**> **H**), at (**A**)= (**D**+**R**)= (**Y**+**H**)+**R**, but if **D**=0, then **Y**=**H**=0 also.

In corporate finance, **D** can be positive, zero or *negative* as well, but id **D**<0 the **Y** and **H** won't means as share-holder's additional contribution to corporate. It might be just transferring non taxable items inside the same group of companies, as permitted by the tax and legal system.

# British Petroleum's *Artistic*[165], Finance

Please look at visuals af pages **109-119**, to show how we build finance architecture construction of British. Petroleum (BP) We can also apply the ideas to any formats.

|   | 2010 | 2009 | (+) | (%) |
|---|------|------|-----|-----|
| c | 125.00% | 101.95% | 23.05% | 22.61% |
| d | 20.00% | 1.08% | 18.92% | 1751.82% |
| f | 25.00% | 30.46% | -5.46% | -17.93% |
| g | 120.00 | 77.38 | 42.62 | 55.07% |
| i | 5.00% | 0.48% | 4.52% | 950.38% |
| j | 30.00 | 38.87 | (8.87) | -22.82% |
| l | 100.00% | 132.22% | -32.22% | -24.37% |
| p | 45.00 | 49.69 | (4.69) | -9.44% |
| q | 100.00% | 63.84% | 36.16% | 56.64% |
| s | 10.00% | -25.48% | 35.48% | -139.24% |
| t | 30.00% | 33.29% | -3.29% | -9.90% |
| v | 55.00% | 59.88% | -4.88% | -8.14% |
| y | 30.00% | 0.00% | 30.00% | #DIV/0! |

By the end of 2010 BP can have 20% sales or revenue growth (**s**). We know that its previous sales or revenue (**S'**)= 273,519 or growing (**s'**)= –25.48% from its two years ago **S"**=367,053. So it is realistic and no big deal, **S=(1+s)S'** =(1+20%) x 273,053= 300,871. *Just like that!*

Then we follow the key-piles and lock-stone ratios to complete all it's **A** to **Z** finance items and **a** to **z** ratios.

## _Technological Mastery_[166] of British Petroleum

If it needs variable portion ($v$)=55%, its variable xpenses ($V$)=$Sv$=300,871x55%= 165,479. So then margin of contribution ($M$)= ($S-V$)= 300,871-165,479= 135,392.

| | | | | | | |
|---|---|---|---|---|---|---|
| 300,871 | 165,479 | | | | | |
| latest | 135,392 | 75,218 | | | | |
| | | 60,174 | 15,044 | | | |
| | | | 45,131 | 13,539 | | |
| | | | | 31,591 | 6,318 | 1,895 |
| previous | | | | | | 4,423 |
| 273,519 | | | | | 25,273 | |

**British Petroleum-10**

| | | | | | |
|---|---|---|---|---|---|
| 57,667 | 103,424 | 253,772 | 126,886 | 82,739 | 55,160 |
| 25,073 | | | | | 27,580 |
| 20,685 | | | | 44,147 | |
| | 150,348 | | 126,886 | 101,613 | |
| | | | | 25,273 | |

If it needs fixed portion ($f$)=25%, its fixed xpenses ($F$)=$Sf$=300,871x25%=75,218. So then its operational surplus ($O$)= ($M-F$)=135,392-75,218= 60,174.

If it also needs investment or financial portion ($i$)=5%, its investment or financial xpenses ($I$)=$Si$= 300,871x5%=15,044. So then its before tax income ($B$)= ($O-I$)=60,174-15,044=45,131. _It's Paccioli's rule._

We just translating it the visual finance architecture, geometric and algebra form, to make it better understood.

# British Petroleum and Finance *Shamanism*[167]

If it needs tax rate (**t**)=30%, its tax paid (**T**)= **Bt**=45,131x30%=13,539. So then its after tax income (**A**)= (**B-T**)= 45,131-13,539=31,591.

|   | 2010 | 2009 | (+) | (%) |
|---|------|------|-----|-----|
| a | 12.45% | 7.10% | 5.35% | 75.28% |
| b | 17.78% | 10.65% | 7.14% | 67.03% |
| e | 19.92% | 16.31% | 3.60% | 22.09% |
| h | 4.35% | 0.00% | 4.35% | #DIV/0! |
| k | 69.70% | 14.06% | 55.64% | 395.79% |
| m | 118.56% | 115.91% | 2.65% | 2.28% |
| n | 8.40% | 6.06% | 2.34% | 38.59% |
| o | 23.71% | 11.20% | 12.51% | 111.73% |
| r | 9.96% | 7.03% | 2.93% | 41.75% |
| u | 24.87% | 19.50% | 5.38% | 27.58% |
| w | 45.00 | (11.17) | 56.17 | -502.75% |
| x | 65.21% | 44.15% | 21.06% | 47.69% |
| z | 21.74% | 17.95% | 3.79% | 21.09% |

If it also needs dividend payout rate (**d**)=20%, its dividend paid (**D**)=**Ad**=31,591x20%=6,318. So then its retained earnings (**R**)= (**A-D**)= 31,591-6,318=25,273.

If it also needs yielding tax of dividend (**y**)=30%, its yielding tax paid (**Y**)=**Dy**=6,318x30%=1,895. So then its home taken dividend (**H**)= (**D-Y**)=6,318-1,895=4,423 They are very simple for Income Statement items.

# *Ability to Collect* [168] at British Petroleum Architecture

Now, let's try its Balanche-sheet items. Its utilized capital at the beginning (**U**) is the equity at the end of the previous year (**E'**), so then (**U=E'**), then **E=(U+R)=** 101,613 +25,273=126,886. It's still follow *Paccioli's rule*.

|   | 2010 | 2009 | (+) | (%) |
|---|---|---|---|---|
| A | 31,591 | 16,759 | 14,832 | 88.50% |
| B | 45,131 | 25,124 | 20,007 | 79.63% |
| C | 103,424 | 60,475 | 42,949 | 71.02% |
| D | 6,318 | 181 | 6,137 | 3390.77% |
| E | 126,886 | 101,613 | 25,273 | 24.87% |
| F | 75,218 | 83,321 | (8,103) | -9.73% |
| G | 55,160 | 35,204 | 19,956 | 56.69% |
| H | 4,423 | - | 4,423 | #DIV/0! |
| I | 15,044 | 1,302 | 13,742 | 1055.42% |
| J | 20,685 | 29,531 | (8,846) | -29.96% |
| K | 25,073 | 8,339 | 16,734 | 200.67% |
| L | 126,886 | 134,355 | (7,469) | -5.56% |
| M | 135,392 | 109,747 | 25,645 | 23.37% |

If it needs better stability, its leverage or gearing ratio (**l**)=100%, its liability at the total (**L**)=**El**=126,886x 100%=126,886. So then its wealth or total asset (**W**)= (**E+L**)=126,886+126,886=253,772.

Aimed procured inventory days (**p**)=45, its procured inventory (**P**)=(**Vp**/360)=165,479x45/360= 20,685.

# British Petroleum Finance's *Qin Greatness*[169]

Let's deal with the current ratio $(c)=(C/X)=125\%$ and quick or acid test ratio $(q)=(C-P)/X=100\%$ concepts.

|   | 2010 | 2009 | (+) | (%) |
|---|------|------|-----|-----|
| N | 150,348 | 175,493 | (25,145) | -14.33% |
| O | 60,174 | 26,426 | 33,748 | 127.71% |
| P | 20,685 | 22,605 | (1,920) | -8.49% |
| Q | 44,147 | 75,035 | (30,888) | -41.17% |
| R | 25,273 | 16,578 | 8,695 | 52.45% |
| S | 300,871 | 273,519 | 27,352 | 10.00% |
| T | 13,539 | 8,365 | 5,174 | 61.86% |
| U | 101,613 | 85,035 | 16,578 | 19.50% |
| V | 165,479 | 163,772 | 1,707 | 1.04% |
| W | 253,772 | 235,968 | 17,804 | 7.55% |
| X | 82,739 | 59,320 | 23,419 | 39.48% |
| Y | 1,895 | - | 1,895 | #DIV/0! |
| Z | 27,580 | 24,116 | 3,464 | 14.36% |

Since $c=(C/X)$ then $C=Xc$ and since $q=(C-P)/X$, then $(C-P)=Xq$ or $C=Xq+P$. It means that $(C=C)$ or $Xc=Xq+P$, so $(Xc-Xq)=P$ or $X(c-q)=P$, then $X=P/(c-q)=20,685/(125\%-100\%)=(20,685/25\%)=82,739$.

So, $C=Xc=82,739\times125\%=103,424$ and the quoted long-term debt $(Q)=(L-X)=126,886-82,739=44,147$. If it needs good or trade account payable days $(g)=120$, its good payable $(G)=(Vg/360)=165,479\times120/360=55,160$.

# The Finance *Rendering*[170] of British Petroleum

So then its zero trade related xpress debt that must be paid quickly $(Z)= (X-G)$=82,739-55,160= 27,580.

| 273,519 | 163,772 | | | | | |
|---|---|---|---|---|---|---|
| latest | 109,747 | 83,321 | | | | |
| | | 26,426 | 1,302 | | | |
| | | | 25,124 | 8,365 | | |
| | | | | 16,759 | 181 | - |
| previous | | | | | | - |
| 367,053 | | | | | 16,578 | |

**British Petroleum-09**

| 8,339 | 60,475 | 235,968 | 134,355 | 59,320 | 35,204 |
|---|---|---|---|---|---|
| 29,531 | | | | | 24,116 |
| 22,605 | | | | 75,035 | |
| | 175,493 | | 101,613 | 85,035 | |
| | | | | 16,578 | |

If it also needs job trade account receivable days $(j)$=30, its job trade account receivables $(J)=(Sj/360)$= 300,871x30/360=25,073. So then its kind of cash $(K)= (C-J-P)$=103,424-25,073-20,685=57,667. *It's a moderate one.*

So then its total non current, fix and intangible assets $(N)= (W-C)$=253,772-103,424=150,348.

Mission accomplished, the finance algebra has identified all **A** to **Z** financial architecture items, coherence with *IFRS* standards, and finance architecture made easy. Is it easier? Please ask all world leading *finance professors*!

# British Petroleum *Presentation Techniques*[171]

We shall analyze this suggested British Petroleum finance architecture blue-print! Not necessary, but we do!

| | | | | | | |
|---|---|---|---|---|---|---|
| 367,053 | 266,982 | | | | | |
| latest | 100,071 | 64,832 | | | | |
| | | 35,239 | 956 | | | |
| | | | 34,283 | 12,617 | | |
| | | | | 21,666 | 509 | - |
| previous | | | | | | - |
| #REF! | | | | | 21,157 | |

**British Petroleum-08**

| | | | | | |
|---|---|---|---|---|---|
| 8,197 | 54,279 | 228,238 | 136,935 | 69,793 | 33,644 |
| 29,261 | | | | | 36,149 |
| 16,821 | | | | 67,142 | |
| | 173,959 | | 91,303 | 70,146 | |
| | | | | 21,157 | |

The-26 *IFRS*' (*International Finance Reporting Standard*'s) ratios consist of 13 financial architecture key-piles[33] and 13 others locked-stones[34]. The-13 key-piles are:

01: **c**= Current ratio= $(C/X)$=103,424/82,739=**125.00%**

02: **d**= Dividend paid portion to after tax= $(D/A)$= 6,318/31,591= **20.00%**, *it's sharp!!*

03: **f**= Fix expenses portion to revenue= $(F/S)$= 75,218/300,871= **25.00%**, *it's sharp!!*

04: **g**= Goods or trade account payable days= $(360G/V)$= 360x55,160/165,479=**120.00**, *it's sharp!!*

# _Distribute Resources[172]_ of British Petroleum Finance

05: **i**= Investment or financial portion to revenue= **(I/S)**=
15,044/300,871=**5.00%**, _it's sharp!!_
06: **j**= Job or trade account receivable days= (360**J/S**)=
360x25,073/300,871=**30.00**, _it's sharp!!_

|   | 2009 | 2008 | (+) | (%) |
|---|---|---|---|---|
| c | 101.95% | 77.77% | 24.18% | 31.09% |
| d | 1.08% | 2.35% | -1.27% | -54.03% |
| f | 30.46% | 17.66% | 12.80% | 72.47% |
| g | 77.38 | 45.37 | 32.02 | 70.58% |
| i | 0.48% | 0.26% | 0.22% | 82.77% |
| j | 38.87 | 28.70 | 10.17 | 35.43% |
| l | 132.22% | 149.98% | -17.76% | -11.84% |
| p | 49.69 | 22.68 | 27.01 | 119.08% |
| q | 63.84% | 53.67% | 10.17% | 18.95% |
| s | -25.48% | | | |
| t | 33.29% | 36.80% | -3.51% | -9.53% |
| v | 59.88% | 72.74% | -12.86% | -17.68% |
| y | 0.00% | 0.00% | 0.00% | #DIV/0! |

07: **l**= Leverage or gearing = debt equity ratio= _DER_=
**(L/E)**=126,886/126,886=**100.00%**, _it's sharp!!_
08: **p**= Procurred inventory days= (360**P/V**)=360x20,685
/165,479=**45.00**, _it's sharp!!_
09: **q**= Quick or acid test ratio= **(C-P)/X**=(103,424-20,685)
/82,739=**100.00%**, _it's sharp!!_

# British Petroleum's *Imhotep[173] Stability* go Eternity

10: **s**= Sales or revenue growth to previous= $(S/S'-1)$=
300,871/273,519-1=**10.00%**, *it's sharp!!*

|   | 2009 | 2008 | (+) | (%) |
|---|------|------|-----|-----|
| a | 7.10% | 9.49% | -2.39% | -25.18% |
| b | 10.65% | 15.02% | -4.37% | -29.12% |
| e | 16.31% | 23.17% | -6.86% | -29.59% |
| h | 0.00% | 0.00% | 0.00% | #DIV/0! |
| k | 14.06% | 11.74% | 2.31% | 19.69% |
| m | 115.91% | 160.82% | -44.91% | -27.92% |
| n | 6.06% | 5.76% | 0.30% | 5.15% |
| o | 11.20% | 15.44% | -4.24% | -27.47% |
| r | 7.03% | 9.27% | -2.24% | -24.21% |
| u | 19.50% | 30.16% | -10.67% | -35.36% |
| w | (11.17) | (6.01) | (5.16) | 85.77% |
| x | 44.15% | 50.97% | -6.82% | -13.37% |
| z | 17.95% | 26.40% | -8.45% | -32.01% |

11: **t**= Tax rate or portion to before tax earnings= $(T/B)$=
13,539/60,174=**30.00%**, *it's sharp!!*

12: **v**= Variable expenses portion to revenue= $(V/S)$=
165,479/300,871=**55.00%**, *it's sharp!!*

13: **y**= Yielding tax of the dividend paid= $(Y/D)$=
1,895/6,318= **30.00%**, *it's sharp!!*

All 13 (thirteen) *key-pile* finance architecture ratios can be
set sharp, and guaranteed to perform accurately sharp

# Finance *Architecture Capabilities* of British Petroleum[174]

The 13 (thirteen) *locked-stone* finance architecture ratios just a derivative of its *key-piles* ratio and not sharp.

|   | 2009 | 2008 | (+) | (%) |
|---|------|------|-----|-----|
| A | 16,759 | 21,666 | (4,907) | -22.65% |
| B | 25,124 | 34,283 | (9,159) | -26.72% |
| C | 60,475 | 54,279 | 6,196 | 11.42% |
| D | 181.00 | 509.00 | (328) | -64.44% |
| E | 101,613 | 91,303 | 10,310 | 11.29% |
| F | 83,321 | 64,832 | 18,489 | 28.52% |
| G | 35,204 | 33,644 | 1,560 | 4.64% |
| H | - | - | - | #DIV/0! |
| I | 1,302 | 956 | 346 | 36.19% |
| J | 29,531 | 29,261 | 270 | 0.92% |
| K | 8,339 | 8,197 | 142 | 1.73% |
| L | 134,355 | 136,935 | (2,580) | -1.88% |
| M | 109,747 | 100,071 | 9,676 | 9.67% |

01: **a**= After tax return on asset= (**A/W**)= 31,591 /253,772=**12.45%**

02: **b**= Before tax return on asset= (**B/W**)= 45,131 /253,772=**17.78%**

03: **e**= Equity return= return on equity= *ROE*= (**R/E**)= 25,273/126,886=**19.92%**

04: **h**= Home taken dividend to utilized equity= (**H/U**)= 4,423/101,613=**4.35%**

# British Petroleum for *Creative* Financial *Architects*[175]

05. **k**= Kind of cash liquidity ratio= (**K/X**)=57,667 /82,739
   =**30.30%**

|   | 2009 | 2008 | (+) | (%) |
|---|------|------|-----|-----|
| N | 175,493 | 173,959 | 1,534 | 0.88% |
| O | 26,426 | 35,239 | (8,813) | -25.01% |
| P | 22,605 | 16,821 | 5,784 | 34.39% |
| Q | 75,035 | 67,142 | 7,893 | 11.76% |
| R | 16,578 | 21,157 | (4,579) | -21.64% |
| S | 273,519 | 367,053 | (93,534) | -25.48% |
| T | 8,365 | 12,617 | (4,252) | -33.70% |
| U | 85,035 | 70,146 | 14,889 | 21.23% |
| V | 163,772 | 266,982 | (103,210) | -38.66% |
| W | 235,968 | 228,238 | 7,730 | 3.39% |
| X | 59,320 | 69,793 | (10,473) | -15.01% |
| Y | - | - | - | #DIV/0! |
| Z | 24,116 | 36,149 | (12,033) | -33.29% |

06. **m**= Market-run or asset turn-over= *ATO*= (**S/W**)=
   300,871/253,772=**118.56%**
07. **n**= NPM= net profit margin= (**R/S**)=25,273 /300,871
   =**8.40%**
08. **o**= Operational surplus to asset return=
   (**O/W**)=60,174/253,772=**20.00%**
09. **r**= Return of net earnings on assets= *ROA*= (**R/W**)=
   25,273/253,772=**9.96%**

# Finance *Anthropometric*[176] for British Petroleum

The remaining 4 (four) locked-stone finance architecture ratios are as follow:

10: **u**= Utilized return on starting equity= **(R/U)**= 25,273 /101,613=**24.87%**

11: **w**= Working capital days required= **(g-p-j)**= 120.00-45.00-30.00=**45.00**, *supplier financed!*

12: **x**= Xpress or current to total debt portion= **(X/L)**= 82,739/126,886=**65.21%**

13: **z**= Zero trade liability portion of total debts= **(Z/L)**= 27,580/126,886= **21.74%**

*Why this finance architecture approach is new?* Because it use visuals and graphics (geometry) to make shorter and sharper finance algebra calculations.

*Is there any literature in finance architecture?* No, because thousand of them deals nothing with architecture, they just borrowing the name, but not using its substance.

*Don't they already famous and accepted world-wide?* No architectural authority ever approve them. Let the authorized body decide: which one is a better architecture in financial field? Which one is easier and more beneficial? To judge this matter, we need juries who are qualified in both fields, not just finance consultant who knows no arts.

*How about yourself?* Are you just an architect? Or just a finance expert? Did you know both fields well?

*How about this book so far?* Did you learn some here? Is that easy? Is this useful? Is it already simplifying? We're talking about the concept, but not the skill yet. Know finance architecture is a great thing, but making good decision is another thing. It needs some experiences, but *common sense* definitely needed, it makes them *stronger*!!

# CHAPTER X: Accounting *Hues* and *Colors*

The annual corporate money in-flow is the sales or revenue (**S**) and its real operational surplus (**O**), so then (**O/S**) is the first important profit margin for the business.

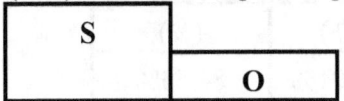

After pay investment or finance cost (**I**), it gets before tax income (**B**), so (**B/S**) is profit margin of leader.

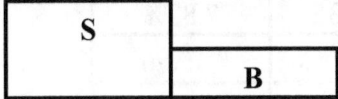

After pay its tax paid (**T**), it gets after tax income (**A**), so (**A/S**) is corporate profit margin for its main owner.

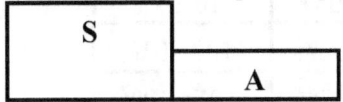

After pay its dividend (**D**), it gets retained earnings ( **R**), so (**R/S**) is corporate  profit margin for its investor.

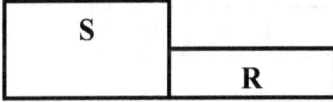

Share-holder also measured its home taken dividend (**H**), so (**H/S**) is profit margin for its short-term player.

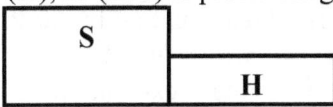

It depends on the people's aim and their position.

# Hyundai Finance *Changdeok*[177] Architecture

Please look at visuals af pages **121-133**, to show how we build finance architecture construction of Hyundai Incorporated We can also apply the ideas to any formats.

|   | 2010 | 2009 | (+) | (%) |
|---|---|---|---|---|
| c | 120.00% | 64.99% | 55.01% | 84.63% |
| d | 20.00% | 0.00% | 20.00% | #DIV/0! |
| f | 10.00% | 10.02% | -0.02% | -0.23% |
| g | 60.00 | 55.65 | 4.35 | 7.82% |
| i | 5.00% | 0.00% | 5.00% | #DIV/0! |
| j | 21.00 | 24.36 | (3.36) | -13.78% |
| l | 100.00% | 60.91% | 39.09% | 64.19% |
| p | 18.00 | 20.03 | (2.03) | -10.13% |
| q | 100.00% | 49.48% | 50.52% | 102.10% |
| s | 10.00% | -1.03% | 11.03% | -1074.12% |
| t | 30.00% | 21.68% | 8.32% | 38.37% |
| v | 75.00% | 78.11% | -3.11% | -3.98% |
| y | 30.00% | #DIV/0! | #DIV/0! | #DIV/0! |

By the end of 2010 Hyundai can have 10% sales or revenue growth (**s**). We know that its previous sales or revenue (**S'**)= 31,859 or growing (**s'**)= -1.03% from its two years ago S"=31,190. So it is realistic and no big deal, **S**=(1+**s**)**S'** =(1+10%) x 31,859= 35,045. *Just like that!*

Then we follow the key-piles and lock-stone ratios to complete all it's **A** to **Z** finance items and **a** to **z** ratios.

If it needs variable portion $(v)$=75%, its variable xpenses $(V)=Sv$=35,045x75%=26,284. So then margin of contribution $(M)= (S-V)$=35,045-26,285=8,761.

| 35,045 | 26,284 | | | | | |
|---|---|---|---|---|---|---|
| latest | 8,761 | 3,505 | | | | |
| | | 5,257 | 1,752 | | | |
| | | | 3,505 | 1,051 | | |
| | | | | 2,453 | 491 | 147 |
| previous | | | | | | 343 |
| 31,859 | | | | | 1,963 | |

**Hyundai-10**

| 4,527 | 7,885 | 47,983 | 23,992 | 6,571 | 4,381 |
|---|---|---|---|---|---|
| 2,044 | | | | | 2,190 |
| 1,314 | | | | 17,421 | |
| | 40,098 | | 23,992 | 22,029 | |
| | | | | 1,963 | |

If it needs fixed portion $(f)$=10%, its fixed xpenses $(F)=Sf$=35,045x10%=3,505. So then its operational surplus $(O)= (M-F)$=8,761-3,505= 5,257.

If it also needs investment or financial portion $(i)$=5%, its investment or financial xpenses $(I)=Si$= 35,045x5%=1,752. So then its before tax income $(B)= (O-I)$=5,257-1,752=3,505. *It's Paccioli's rule.*

We just translating it the visual finance architecture, geometric and algebra form, to make it better understood.

## *Han's Dam*[179] Finance at Hyundai

If it needs tax rate ($t$)=30%, its tax paid ($T$)= $Bt$=3.505x30%=1,051. So then its after tax income ($A$)= ($B-T$)= 3,505-1,051=2,453.

|   | 2010 | 2009 | (+) | . (%) |
|---|---|---|---|---|
| a | 5.11% | 8.35% | -3.24% | -38.81% |
| b | 7.30% | 10.67% | -3.36% | -31.54% |
| e | 8.18% | 13.44% | -5.26% | -39.15% |
| h | 1.56% | 0.00% | 1.56% | #DIV/0! |
| k | 68.89% | 25.32% | 43.57% | 172.04% |
| m | 73.04% | 89.88% | -16.84% | -18.74% |
| n | 5.60% | 9.30% | -3.70% | -39.76% |
| o | 10.96% | 10.67% | 0.29% | 2.70% |
| r | 4.09% | 8.35% | -4.26% | -51.05% |
| u | 8.91% | 15.53% | -6.62% | -42.64% |
| w | 21.00 | 11.26 | 9.74 | 86.43% |
| x | 27.39% | 66.51% | -39.12% | -58.82% |
| z | 9.13% | 37.84% | -28.71% | -75.87% |

If it also needs dividend payout rate ($d$)=20%, its dividend paid ($D$)=$Ad$=2,453x20%=491. So then its retained earnings ($R$)= ($A-D$)=2,453-491=1,963.

If it also needs yielding tax of dividend ($y$)=30%, its yielding tax paid ($Y$)=$Dy$=491x30%=147. So then its home taken dividend ($H$)= ($D-Y$)=491-147=343

They are very simple for Income Statement items.

# Panmunjom[180] Accounting at Hyundai

Now, let's try its Balanche-sheet items. Its utilized capital at the beginning (**U**) is the equity at the end of the previous year (**E'**), so then (**U=E'**), then **E=(U+R)**= 22,029+1,963=23,992. It's still follow *Paccioli's rule*.

|   | 2010 | 2009 | (+) | (%) |
|---|------|------|-----|-----|
| A | 2,453 | 2,962 | (508) | -17.16% |
| B | 3,505 | 3,781 | (277) | -7.32% |
| C | 7,885 | 5,800 | 2,085 | 35.95% |
| D | 491 | - | 491 | #DIV/0! |
| E | 23,992 | 22,029 | 1,963 | 8.91% |
| F | 3,505 | 3,193 | 311 | 9.75% |
| G | 4,381 | 3,847 | 534 | 13.88% |
| H | 343 | - | 343 | #DIV/0! |
| I | 1,752 | - | 1,752 | #DIV/0! |
| J | 1,314 | 2,156 | (841) | -39.03% |
| K | 2,044 | 2,260 | (215) | -9.54% |
| L | 23,992 | 13,417 | 10,574 | 78.81% |
| M | 8,761 | 6,975 | 1,787 | 25.62% |

If it needs better stability, its leverage or gearing ratio (**l**)=100%, its liability at the total (**L**)=**El**=23,992x 100%=23,992. So then its wealth or total asset (**W**)= (**E+L**)=23,992+23,992=47,983.

Aimed procured inventory days (**p**)=18, its procured inventory (**P**)=(**Vp**/360)=26,284x18/360=1,314.

# Hyundai Finance and *Yonsei*[181]

Let's deal with the current ratio $(\mathbf{c})=(\mathbf{C/X})=120\%$ and quick or acid test ratio $(\mathbf{q})=(\mathbf{C-P})/\mathbf{X}=100\%$ concepts.

|   | 2010 | 2009 | (+) | (%) |
|---|---|---|---|---|
| N | 40,098 | 29,646 | 10,452 | 35.25% |
| O | 5,257 | 3,781 | 1,475 | 39.02% |
| P | 1,314 | 1,384 | (70) | -5.08% |
| Q | 17,421 | 4,493 | 12,927 | 287.69% |
| R | 1,963 | 2,962 | (999) | -33.73% |
| S | 35,045 | 31,859 | 3,186 | 10.00% |
| T | 1,051 | 820 | 232 | 28.25% |
| U | 22,029 | 19,068 | 2,962 | 15.53% |
| V | 26,284 | 24,885 | 1,399 | 5.62% |
| W | 47,983 | 35,446 | 12,537 | 35.37% |
| X | 6,571 | 8,924 | (2,353) | -26.36% |
| Y | 147 | - | 147 | #DIV/0! |
| Z | 2,190 | 5,077 | (2,887) | -56.86% |

Since $\mathbf{c}=(\mathbf{C/X})$ then $\mathbf{C=Xc}$ and since $\mathbf{q}=(\mathbf{C-P})/\mathbf{X}$, then $(\mathbf{C-P})=\mathbf{Xq}$ or $\mathbf{C=Xq+P}$. It means that $(\mathbf{C=C})$ or $\mathbf{Xc=Xq+P}$, so $(\mathbf{Xc-Xq})=\mathbf{P}$ or $\mathbf{X(c-q)=P}$, then $\mathbf{X=P}/(\mathbf{c-q})=$ $1,314/(120\%-100\%)=(20,685/20\%)=6,571$.

So, $\mathbf{C=Xc}=6,571\times120\%=7,885$ and the quoted long-term debt $(\mathbf{Q})=(\mathbf{L-X})=23,992-6,571=17,421$. If it needs good or trade account payable  days $(\mathbf{g})=60$, its good payable $(\mathbf{G})=(\mathbf{Vg}/360)=26,284\times60/360=4,381$.

So then its zero trade related xpress debt that must be paid quickly $(\mathbf{Z})= (\mathbf{X}\text{-}\mathbf{G})$=6,571-4,381=2,190.

| | | | | | | |
|---|---|---|---|---|---|---|
| 31,859 | 24,885 | | | | | |
| latest | 6,975 | 3,193 | | | | |
| | | 3,781 | - | | | |
| | | | 3,781 | 820 | | |
| | | | | 2,962 | - | - |
| | | | | | | - |
| previous | | | | | | |
| 32,190 | | | | 2,962 | | |

**Hyundai-09**

| | | | | | |
|---|---|---|---|---|---|
| 2,260 | 5,800 | 35,446 | 13,417 | 8,924 | 3,847 |
| 2,156 | | | | | 5,077 |
| 1,384 | | | | 4,493 | |
| | 29,646 | | 22,029 | 19,068 | |
| | | | | 2,962 | |

If it also needs job trade account receivable days $(\mathbf{j})$=21, its job trade account receivables $(\mathbf{J})=(\mathbf{Sj}/360)$= 35,045x21/360=2,044. So then its kind of cash $(\mathbf{K})= (\mathbf{C}\text{-}\mathbf{J}\text{-}\mathbf{P})$=7,885-2,044-1,314=4,527. *It's a moderate one.*

So then its total non current, fix and intangible assets $(\mathbf{N})= (\mathbf{W}\text{-}\mathbf{C})$=47,983-7,885=40,098.

Mission accomplished, the finance algebra has identified all **A** to **Z** financial architecture items, coherence with *IFRS* standards, and finance architecture made easy. Is it easier? It's minor trait, like *Columbus* egg's case.[183]

# Busan[184] for Finance *Architects* of Hyundai

We shall analyze this suggested Hyundai finance architecture blue-print! Not necessary, but we prove them!

| 32,190 | 25,059 | | | | | |
|---|---|---|---|---|---|---|
| latest | 7,131 | 5,336 | | | | |
| | | 1,795 | - | | | |
| | | | 1,795 | 347 | | |
| | | | | 1,448 | - | - |
| previous | | | | | | - |
| - | | | | | 1,448 | |

**Hyundai-08**

| 1,757 | 6,079 | 32,168 | 12,515 | 7,915 | 2,444 |
|---|---|---|---|---|---|
| 2,513 | | | | | 5,471 |
| 1,809 | | | | 4,600 | |
| | 26,089 | | 19,652 | 18,204 | |
| | | | | 1,448 | |

The-26 *IFRS'* (*International Finance Reporting Standard*'s) ratios consist of 13 financial architecture key-piles[33] and 13 others locked-stones[34]. The-13 key-piles are:

01: **c**= Current ratio= (**C/X**)=7,885/6,571=**120.00%**

02: **d**= Dividend paid portion to after tax= (**D/A**)= 491/2,453= **20.00%**, *it's sharp!!*

03: **f**= Fix expenses portion to revenue= (**F/S**)= 3,505/35,045= **10.00%**, *it's sharp!!*

04: **g**= Goods or trade account payable days= (360**G/V**)= 360x4,381/26,284=**60.00**, *it's sharp!!*

# *Incheon*[185] **Accounting at Hyundai**

05: **i**= Investment or financial portion to revenue= **(I/S)**=
    1,752/35,045=**5.00%**, *it's sharp!!*

06: **j**= Job or trade account receivable days= (360**J/S**)=
    360x2,044/35,045=**21.00**, *it's sharp!!*

|   | 2009 | 2008 | (+) | (%) |
|---|---|---|---|---|
| c | 64.99% | 76.80% | -11.81% | -15.38% |
| d | 0.00% | 0.00% | 0.00% | #DIV/0! |
| f | 10.02% | 16.58% | -6.55% | -39.54% |
| g | 55.65 | 35.11 | 20.54 | 58.51% |
| i | 0.00% | 0.00% | 0.00% | #DIV/0! |
| j | 24.36 | 28.11 | (3.75) | -13.35% |
| l | 60.91% | 63.68% | -2.78% | -4.36% |
| p | 20.03 | 25.99 | (5.96) | -22.93% |
| q | 49.48% | 53.95% | -4.47% | -8.28% |
| s | -1.03% | | | |
| t | 21.68% | 19.34% | 2.34% | 12.12% |
| v | 78.11% | 77.85% | 0.26% | 0.34% |
| y | #DIV/0! | #DIV/0! | #DIV/0! | #DIV/0! |

07: **l**= Leverage or gearing = debt equity ratio= *DER*=
    (**L/E**)=23,992/23,992=**100.00%**, *it's sharp!!*

08: **p**= Procurred inventory days= (360**P/V**)=360x2,044
    /26,284=**18.00**, *it's sharp!!*

09: **q**= Quick or acid test ratio= **(C-P)/X**=(7,885-1,314)
    /6,571=**100.00%**, *it's sharp!!*

# Hyundai Finance *Gwangju Kimchi*[186]

10: **s**= Sales or revenue growth to previous= (S/S'-1)=
35,045/31,859-1=**10.00%**, *it's sharp!!*

|   | 2009 | 2008 | (+) | (%) |
|---|------|------|-----|-----|
| a | 8.35% | 4.50% | 3.85% | 85.62% |
| b | 10.67% | 5.58% | 5.09% | 91.17% |
| e | 13.44% | 7.37% | 6.08% | 82.47% |
| h | 0.00% | 0.00% | 0.00% | #DIV/0! |
| k | 25.32% | 22.19% | 3.13% | 14.11% |
| m | 89.88% | 100.07% | -10.19% | -10.18% |
| n | 9.30% | 4.50% | 4.80% | 106.66% |
| o | 10.67% | 5.58% | 5.09% | 91.17% |
| r | 8.35% | 4.50% | 3.85% | 85.62% |
| u | 15.53% | 7.95% | 7.58% | 95.28% |
| w | 11.26 | (18.99) | 30.25 | -159.32% |
| x | 66.51% | 63.24% | 3.27% | 5.17% |
| z | 37.84% | 43.72% | -5.88% | -13.44% |

11: **t**= Tax rate or portion to before tax earnings= (T/B)=
1,051/3,505=**30.00%**, *it's sharp!!*
12: **v**= Variable expenses portion to revenue= (V/S)=
26,284/35,045=**75.00%**, *it's sharp!!*
13: **y**= Yielding tax of the dividend paid= (Y/D)=147 /491=
**30.00%**, *it's sharp!!*
All  13 (thirteen) *key-pile* finance architecture ratios
can be set sharp, and guaranteed to perform accurately sharp

# Hyundai Accounting *Goguryeo*[187]

The 13 (thirteen) *locked-stone* finance architecture ratios just a derivative of its *key-piles* ratio and not sharp.

|   | 2009 | 2008 | (+) | (%) |
|---|------|------|-----|-----|
| A | 2,962 | 1,448 | 1,514 | 104.54% |
| B | 3,781 | 1,795 | 1,986 | 110.66% |
| C | 5,800 | 6,079 | (279) | -4.59% |
| D | - | - | - | #DIV/0! |
| E | 22,029 | 19,652 | 2,377 | 12.09% |
| F | 3,193 | 5,336 | (2,143) | -40.16% |
| G | 3,847 | 2,444 | 1,403 | 57.41% |
| H | - | - | - | #DIV/0! |
| I | - | - | - | #DIV/0! |
| J | 2,156 | 2,513 | (358) | -14.24% |
| K | 2,260 | 1,757 | 503 | 28.65% |
| L | 13,417 | 12,515 | 902 | 7.20% |
| M | 6,975 | 7,131 | (157) | -2.20% |

01: **a**= After tax return on asset= **(A/W)**=2,453/47,983 =**5.11%**

02: **b**= Before tax return on asset= **(B/W)**=3,505/47,983 =**7.30%**

03: **e**= Equity return= return on equity= *ROE*= **(R/E)**= 1,963 /47,983=**8.18%**

04: **h**= Home taken dividend to utilized equity= **(H/U)**= 343/22,029=**1.56%**

## *Baekje*[188] Finance of Hyundai

05. **k**= Kind of cash liquidity ratio= **(K/X)**=4,527/6,571
    =**68.89%**

|   | 2009 | 2008 | (+) | (%) |
|---|---|---|---|---|
| N | 29,646 | 26,089 | 3,558 | 13.64% |
| O | 3,781 | 1,795 | 1,986 | 110.66% |
| P | 1,384 | 1,809 | (425) | -23.47% |
| Q | 4,493 | 4,600 | (107) | -2.32% |
| R | 2,962 | 1,448 | 1,514 | 104.54% |
| S | 31,859 | 32,190 | (330) | -1.03% |
| T | 820 | 347 | 473 | 136.18% |
| U | 19,068 | 18,204 | 863 | 4.74% |
| V | 24,885 | 25,059 | (174) | -0.69% |
| W | 35,446 | 32,168 | 3,278 | 10.19% |
| X | 8,924 | 7,915 | 1,009 | 12.74% |
| Y | - | - | - | #DIV/0! |
| Z | 5,077 | 5,471 | (394) | -7.21% |

06. **m**= Market-run or asset turn-over= *ATO*= **(S/W)**=
    35,045/47,983=**73.04%**

07. **n**= NPM= net profit margin= **(R/S)**=1,963/35,045
    =**5.60%**

08. **o**= Operational surplus to asset return= **(O/W)**=5,257
    /47,983=**10.96%**

09. **r**= Return of net earnings on assets= *ROA*= **(R/W)**=
    1,963/47,983=**4.09%**

## _Silla_[189] **Accounting at Hyundai**

The remaining 4 (four) locked-stone finance architecture ratios are as follow:

10: **u**= Utilized return on starting equity= (**R/U**)= 1,963 /22,029=**8.91%**

11: **w**= Working capital days required= (**g-p-j**)= 60.00-18.00-21.00=**21.00**, _supplier financed!_

12: **x**= Xpress or current to total debt portion= (**X/L**)= 6,751/23,992=**27.39%**

13: **z**= Zero trade liability portion of total debts= (**Z/L**)= 2,190/23,992= **9.13%**

_Why this book can make finance architecture so easy?_ Because it stream-lining various accounting items in **IFRS** format by it's **A** to **Z** items and **a** to **z** finance ratios,.

_Why it is significantly different than other finance?_ Because it formats the uncontrollable various accounting items, to be a compact interactive finance architecture.

_Why other people never even think about it?_ Because they never see Paccioli's law as just a method of thinking. They assume it exactly as solar and earth orbitals.

_Is it fair to set different finance constellation?_ No, it takes a genius to propose better paradigm like Galileo or Einstein. It's always risky. Few finance conservatives had tried hard to examine the worse method so far. They do not want any novice easily get real essence faster. _They'll fight!_

_Why should we defend this?_ Many people have the right for better finance and they must understand it quickly!

_Is it true?_ Prove it, let every body chose the best. Is finance still difficult? Do they get better finance decision? Are the 13 real world-class company finance improved?

_How's if it comparted to Nobel laureates?_ We tell the best way for finance, but they are best men at old-ways.

The real corporate money invested is the utilized equity (**U**) and its real operational surplus (**O**), so then (**O/U**) is the first important profit margin for the business.

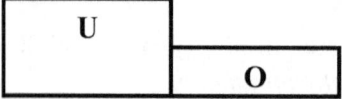

After pay investment or finance cost (**I**), it gets before tax income (**B**), so (**B/U**)= return on equity of leader

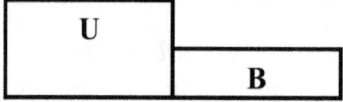

After pay its tax paid (**T**), it gets after tax income (**A**), so (**A/U**)= return on equity for its main owner.

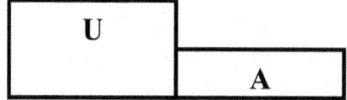

After pay its dividend (**D**), it gets retained earnings ( **R**), so (**R/U**)= return on equity for its investor.

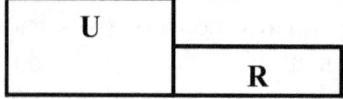

Share-holder also measured its home taken dividend (**H**), so (**H/U**)= return on equity for its short-term player.

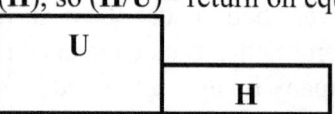

It depends on the people's aim and their position.

# Finance *Mercedes Plant*[191] **Architecture of Benz**

Please look at visuals af pages **134-146**, to show how we build finance architecture construction of Daimler Incorporated We can also apply the ideas to any formats.

|   | 2010 | 2009 | (+) | (%) |
|---|---|---|---|---|
| c | 120.00% | 31.08% | 88.92% | 286.08% |
| d | 20.00% | 0.00% | 20.00% | #DIV/0! |
| f | 10.00% | 17.80% | -7.80% | -43.81% |
| g | 120.00 | 25.22 | 94.78 | 375.76% |
| i | 2.00% | -2.88% | 4.88% | -169.48% |
| j | 10.00 | 11.06 | (1.06) | -9.56% |
| l | 100.00% | 269.38% | -169.38% | -62.88% |
| p | 30.00 | 39.41 | (9.41) | -23.88% |
| q | 100.00% | 13.42% | 86.58% | 645.38% |
| s | 10.00% | -25.92% | 35.92% | -138.58% |
| t | 30.00% | -9.19% | 39.19% | -426.48% |
| v | 80.00% | 94.33% | -14.33% | -15.19% |
| y | 30.00% | #DIV/0! | #DIV/0! | #DIV/0! |

By the end of 2010 Daimler can have 10% sales or revenue growth (**s**). We know that its previous sales or revenue (**S'**)=47,177 or growing (**s'**)= -25.92% from its two years ago **S"**=63,682. So it is realistic and no big deal, **S**=(1+**s**)**S'** =(1+10%) x 47,177= 51,895. *Just like that!*

Then we follow the key-piles and lock-stone ratios to complete all it's **A** to **Z** finance items and **a** to **z** ratios.

# Benz Accounting *DaimlerChrysler*[192] Architecture

If it needs variable portion (**v**)=80%, its variable xpenses (**V**)=**Sv**=51,895x80%=41,516. So then margin of contribution (**M**)= (**S-V**)=51,895-41,516=10,379.

| | | | | | | |
|---|---|---|---|---|---|---|
| 51,895 | 41,516 | | | | | |
| latest | 10,379 | 5,189 | | | | |
| | | 5,189 | 1,038 | | | |
| | | | 4,152 | 1,245 | | |
| | | | | 2,906 | 581 | 174 |
| previous | | | | | | 407 |
| 47,177 | | | | | 2,325 | |

**Daimler-Benz-10**

| | | | | | |
|---|---|---|---|---|---|
| 15,857 | 20,758 | 44,428 | 22,214 | 17,298 | 13,839 |
| 1,442 | | | | | 3,460 |
| 3,460 | | | | 4,916 | |
| | 23,670 | | 22,214 | 19,889 | |
| | | | | 2,325 | |

If it needs fixed portion (**f**)=10%, its fixed xpenses (**F**)=**Sf**=51,895x10%=5,189. So then its operational surplus (**O**)= (**M-F**)=10,379-5,189= 5,189.

If it also needs investment or financial portion (**i**)=2%, its investment or financial xpenses (**I**)=**Si**= 51,895x2%=1,038. So then its before tax income (**B**)= (**O-I**)=5,189-1,038=4,152. *It's Paccioli's rule.*

We just translating it the visual finance architecture, geometric and algebra form, to make it better understood.

If it needs tax rate (**t**)=30%, its tax paid (**T**)= **B**t= 4,152x30%=1,245. So then its after tax income (**A**)= (**B**-**T**)= 4,152-1,245=2,906.

|   | 2010 | 2009 | (+) | (%) |
|---|---|---|---|---|
| a | 6.54% | -6.49% | 13.03% | -200.85% |
| b | 9.34% | -5.94% | 15.28% | -257.31% |
| e | 10.47% | -23.96% | 34.42% | -143.68% |
| h | 2.05% | 0.00% | 2.05% | #DIV/0! |
| k | 91.67% | 8.16% | 83.50% | 1023.09% |
| m | 116.81% | 64.22% | 52.59% | 81.89% |
| n | 4.48% | -10.10% | 14.58% | -144.36% |
| o | 11.68% | -7.79% | 19.47% | -249.97% |
| r | 5.23% | -6.49% | 11.72% | -180.68% |
| u | 11.69% | -19.33% | 31.02% | -160.48% |
| w | 80.00 | (25.25) | 105.25 | -416.88% |
| x | 77.87% | 51.48% | 26.39% | 51.28% |
| z | 15.57% | 45.66% | -30.08% | -65.89% |

If it also needs dividend payout rate (**d**)=20%, its dividend paid (**D**)=**A**d=2,906x20%=581. So then its retained earnings (**R**)= (**A**-**D**)=2,906-581=2,325.

If it also needs yielding tax of dividend (**y**)=30%, its yielding tax paid (**Y**)=**D**y=581x30%=174. So then its home taken dividend (**H**)= (**D**-**Y**)=581-174=407.

They are very simple for Income Statement items.

# *Koliusis Installation*[194] of Benz Accounting

Now, let's try its Balanche-sheet items. Its utilized capital at the beginning (**U**) is the equity at the end of the previous year (**E'**), so then (**U=E'**), then **E=(U+R)**= 19,889+2,325=22,214. It's still follow *Paccioli's rule*.

|   | 2010 | 2009 | (+) | (%) |
|---|---|---|---|---|
| A | 2,906 | (4,765) | 7,671 | -160.99% |
| B | 4,152 | (4,364) | 8,516 | -195.13% |
| C | 20,758 | 8,572 | 12,186 | 142.16% |
| D | 581 | - | 581 | #DIV/0! |
| E | 22,214 | 19,889 | 2,325 | 11.69% |
| F | 5,189 | 8,396 | (3,207) | -38.19% |
| G | 13,839 | 3,118 | 10,721 | 343.83% |
| H | 407 | - | 407 | #DIV/0! |
| I | 1,038 | (1,358) | 2,396 | -176.43% |
| J | 3,460 | 1,449 | 2,011 | 138.76% |
| K | 1,442 | 2,251 | (809) | -35.96% |
| L | 22,214 | 53,576 | (31,362) | -58.54% |
| M | 10,379 | 2,674 | 7,705 | 288.14% |

If it needs better stability, its leverage or gearing ratio (**l**)=100%, its liability at the total (**L**)=**El**=22,214x 100%=22,214. So then its wealth or total asset (**W**)= (**E+L**)=22,214+22,214=44,428.

Aimed procured inventory days (**p**)=30, its procured inventory (**P**)=(**Vp**/360)=41,516x30/360=3,460.

# Benz Finance's *U-bahn*[195] Architecture

Let's deal with the current ratio (**c** )=(**C/X**)=120% and quick or acid test ratio (**q**)=(**C-P**)/**X**=100% concepts.

|   | 2010 | 2009 | (+) | (%) |
|---|------|------|-----|-----|
| N | 23,670 | 64,893 | (41,223) | -63.52% |
| O | 5,189 | (5,722) | 10,911 | -190.69% |
| P | 3,460 | 4,872 | (1,412) | -28.99% |
| Q | 4,916 | 25,997 | (21,081) | -81.09% |
| R | 2,325 | (4,765) | 7,090 | -148.79% |
| S | 51,895 | 47,177 | 4,718 | 10.00% |
| T | 1,245 | 401 | 844 | 210.59% |
| U | 19,889 | 24,654 | (4,765) | -19.33% |
| V | 41,516 | 44,503 | (2,987) | -6.71% |
| W | 44,428 | 73,465 | (29,037) | -39.53% |
| X | 17,298 | 27,579 | (10,281) | -37.28% |
| Y | 174 | - | 174 | #DIV/0! |
| Z | 3,460 | 24,461 | (21,001) | -85.86% |

Since **c**=(**C/X**) then **C=Xc** and since **q**=(**C-P**)/**X**, then (**C-P**)=**Xq** or **C=Xq+P**. It means that (**C=C**) or **Xc=Xq+P**, so (**Xc-Xq**)=**P** or **X(c-q)=P**, then **X=P/(c-q)**= 3,460/(120%-100%)=(3,460/20%)=17,298.

So, **C=Xc**=17,298x120%=20,758 and the quoted long-term debt (**Q**)=(**L-X**)=22,214-17,298=4,916. If it needs good or trade account payable days (**g**)=120, its good payable (**G**)=(**Vg**/360)=41,516x120/360=13,839.

# Accounting *Stäffele*[196] *Stuttgart* of Benz

So then its zero trade related xpress debt that must be paid quickly $(Z)= (X-G)=17{,}298-13{,}839=3{,}460$.

| 47,177 | 44,503 | | | | | |
|---|---|---|---|---|---|---|
| latest | 2,674 | 8,396 | | | | |
| | | (5,722) | (1,358) | | | |
| | | | (4,364) | 401 | | |
| | | | | (4,765) | - | - |
| previous | | | | | | - |
| 63,682 | | | | | (4,765) | |

**Daimler-Benz-09**

| 2,251 | 8,572 | 73,465 | 53,576 | 27,579 | 3,118 |
|---|---|---|---|---|---|
| 1,449 | | | | | 24,461 |
| 4,872 | | | | 25,997 | |
| | 64,893 | | 19,889 | 24,654 | |
| | | | | (4,765) | |

If it also needs job trade account receivable days $(j)=10$, its job trade account receivables $(J)=(Sj/360)= 51{,}895 \times 10/360=1{,}442$. So then its kind of cash $(K)= (C-J-P)=20{,}758-1{,}442-3{,}460=15{,}857$. *It's a conservative one.*

So then its total non current, fix and intangible assets $(N)= (W-C)=44{,}428-20{,}758=23{,}670$.

Mission accomplished, the finance algebra has identified all **A** to **Z** financial architecture items, coherence with *IFRS* standards, and finance architecture made easy. Is it easier? It's minor trait, like *Copernican orbital*[197] case.

# Benz *Kaufhaus Schocken*[198] Finance Architecture

We shall analyze this suggested Daimler finance architecture blue-print! Not necessary, but we prove them!

| 63,682 | 57,064 | | | | | |
|---|---|---|---|---|---|---|
| latest | 6,618 | 7,937 | | | | |
| | | (1,319) | (1,164) | | | |
| | | | (155) | 177 | | |
| | | | | (332) | - | - |
| previous | | | | | | - |
| - | | | | | (332) | |

**Daimler-Benz-08**

| 772 | 8,829 | 68,377 | 45,453 | 21,577 | 3,431 |
|---|---|---|---|---|---|
| 2,024 | | | | | 18,146 |
| 6,033 | | | | 23,876 | |
| | 59,548 | | | 22,924 | 23,256 |
| | | | | | (332) |

The-26 ***IFRS*** (*International Finance Reporting Standard*'s) ratios consist of 13 financial architecture key-piles[33] and 13 others locked-stones[34]. The-13 key-piles are:

01: **c**= Current ratio= $(C/X)$=20,758/17,298=**120.00%**

02: **d**= Dividend paid portion to after tax= $(D/A)$= 581/2,906= **20.00%**, *it's sharp!!*

03: **f**= Fix expenses portion to revenue= $(F/S)$= 5,189/51,895= **10.00%**, *it's sharp!!*

04: **g**= Goods or trade account payable days= $(360G/V)$= 360x13,839/41,516=**120.00**, *it's sharp!!*

# <u>*Gro?stadt triptych*[199]</u> **for Benz Accounting Arts**

05: **i**= Investment or financial portion to revenue= (**I/S**)=
  1,038/51,895=**<u>2.00%</u>**, *it's sharp!!*
06: **j**= Job or trade account receivable days= (360**J/S**)=
  360x1,442/51,895=**<u>10.00</u>**, *it's sharp!!*

|   | 2009 | 2008 | (+) | (%) |
|---|---|---|---|---|
| c | 31.08% | 40.92% | -9.84% | -24.04% |
| d | 0.00% | 0.00% | 0.00% | #DIV/0! |
| f | 17.80% | 12.46% | 5.33% | 42.79% |
| g | 25.22 | 21.65 | 3.58 | 16.53% |
| i | -2.88% | -1.83% | -1.05% | 57.48% |
| j | 11.06 | 11.44 | (0.38) | -3.36% |
| l | 269.38% | 198.28% | 71.10% | 35.86% |
| p | 39.41 | 38.06 | 1.35 | 3.55% |
| q | 13.42% | 12.96% | 0.46% | 3.53% |
| s | -25.92% |  |  |  |
| t | -9.19% | -114.19% | 105.00% | -91.95% |
| v | 94.33% | 89.61% | 4.72% | 5.27% |
| y | #DIV/0! | #DIV/0! | #DIV/0! | #DIV/0! |

07: **l**= Leverage or gearing = debt equity ratio= *DER*=
  (**L/E**)=22,214/22,214=**<u>100.00%</u>**, *it's sharp!!*
08: **p**= Procurred inventory days= (360**P/V**)=360x3,460
  /41,516=**<u>30.00</u>**, *it's sharp!!*
09: **q**= Quick or acid test ratio= (**C-P**)/**X**=(20,758-3,460)
  /17,298=**<u>100.00%</u>**, *it's sharp!!*

10: **s**= Sales or revenue growth to previous= (**S/S'**-1)= 51,895/47,177-1=**10.00%**, *it's sharp!!*

|   | 2009 | 2008 | (+) | (%) |
|---|------|------|-----|-----|
| a | -6.49% | -0.49% | -6.00% | 1235.84% |
| b | -5.94% | -0.23% | -5.71% | 2520.49% |
| e | -23.96% | -1.45% | -22.51% | 1554.25% |
| h | 0.00% | 0.00% | 0.00% | #DIV/0! |
| k | 8.16% | 3.58% | 4.58% | 128.12% |
| m | 64.22% | 93.13% | -28.92% | -31.05% |
| n | -10.10% | -0.52% | -9.58% | 1837.36% |
| o | -7.79% | -1.93% | -5.86% | 303.77% |
| r | -6.49% | -0.49% | -6.00% | 1235.84% |
| u | -19.33% | -1.43% | -17.90% | 1253.86% |
| w | (25.25) | (27.86) | 2.61 | -9.37% |
| x | 51.48% | 47.47% | 4.01% | 8.44% |
| z | 45.66% | 39.92% | 5.73% | 14.36% |

11: **t**= Tax rate or portion to before tax earnings= (**T/B**)= 1,245/4,152=**30.00%**, *it's sharp!!*

12: **v**= Variable expenses portion to revenue= (**V/S**)= 41,516/51,895=**80.00%**, *it's sharp!!*

13: **y**= Yielding tax of the dividend paid= (**Y/D**)=174 /407= **30.00%**, *it's sharp!!*

All 13 (thirteen) *key-pile* finance architecture ratios can be set sharp, and guaranted to perform accurately sharp

# Accounting _Königsbau Passagen_[201] of Benz

The 13 (thirteen) _locked-stone_ finance architecture ratios just a derivative of its _key-piles_ ratio and not sharp.

|   | 2009 | 2008 | (+) | (%) |
|---|------|------|-----|-----|
| A | (4,765) | (332) | (4,433) | 1335.24% |
| B | (4,364) | (155) | (4,209) | 2715.48% |
| C | 8,572 | 8,829 | (257) | -2.91% |
| D | - | - | - | #DIV/0! |
| E | 19,889 | 22,924 | (3,035) | -13.24% |
| F | 8,396 | 7,937 | 459 | 5.78% |
| G | 3,118 | 3,431 | (313) | -9.12% |
| H | - | - | - | #DIV/0! |
| I | (1,358) | (1,164) | (194) | 16.67% |
| J | 1,449 | 2,024 | (575) | -28.41% |
| K | 2,251 | 772 | 1,479 | 191.58% |
| L | 53,576 | 45,453 | 8,123 | 17.87% |
| M | 2,674 | 6,618 | (3,944) | -59.60% |

01: **a**= After tax return on asset= **(A/W)**=2,906/51,895 =**6.54%**

02: **b**= Before tax return on asset= **(B/W)**=5,189/51,895 =**9.34%**

03: **e**= Equity return= return on equity= _ROE_= **(R/E)**= 2,325 /22,214=**10.47%**

04: **h**= Home taken dividend to utilized equity= **(H/U)**= 407/19,889=**2.05%**

## Benz *Weissenhofsiedlung* Finance Architecture

05. **k**= Kind of cash liquidity ratio= **(K/X)**=15,857/17,298
    =**91.67%**

|   | 2009 | 2008 | (+) | (%) |
|---|------|------|-----|-----|
| N | 64,893 | 59,548 | 5,345 | 8.98% |
| O | (5,722) | (1,319) | (4,403) | 333.81% |
| P | 4,872 | 6,033 | (1,161) | -19.24% |
| Q | 25,997 | 23,876 | 2,121 | 8.88% |
| R | (4,765) | (332) | (4,433) | 1335.24% |
| S | 47,177 | 63,682 | (16,505) | -25.92% |
| T | 401 | 177 | 224 | 126.55% |
| U | 24,654 | 23,256 | 1,398 | 6.01% |
| V | 44,503 | 57,064 | (12,561) | -22.01% |
| W | 73,465 | 68,377 | 5,088 | 7.44% |
| X | 27,579 | 21,577 | 6,002 | 27.82% |
| Y | - | - | - | #DIV/0! |
| Z | 24,461 | 18,146 | 6,315 | 34.80% |

06. **m**= Market-run or asset turn-over= *ATO*= **(S/W)**=
    51,895/44,428=**116.81%**
07. **n**= NPM= net profit margin= **(R/S)**=2,325/51,895
    =**4.48%**
08. **o**= Operational surplus to asset return= **(O/W)**=5,189
    /44,428=**4.60%**
09. **r**= Return of net earnings on assets= *ROA*= **(R/W)**=
    2,325/47,983=**5.23%**

# Der *Kriegsbergstrasse*[202] Accounting Architecture

The remaining 4 (four) locked-stone finance architecture ratios are as follow:

10: **u**= Utilized return on starting equity= **(R/U)**= 2,325 /19,889=**11.69%**

11: **w**= Working capital days required= **(g-p-j)**= 120.00-30.00-10.00=**80.00**, *supplier financed!*

12: **x**= Xpress or current to total debt portion= **(X/L)**= 17,298/22,214=**77.87%**

13: **z**= Zero trade liability portion of total debts= **(Z/L)**= 3,460/22,214= **15.57%**

*Why that professional architects never touching the finance architecture before?* They are too busy, learning architecture combining arts, engineering, social behaviour and economy. It takes so much energies and concentration.

*Why finance and accounting people never seriously lear graphics for their finance architecture?* Spatial skills needs different intelligence.than just arithmetic (x,:,+,-). Not so many people good in Cartesian XY and its Calculus.

*Why this makes financial computations short and easy?* Because it translating various accounting items in **IFRS** format by it's **A** to **Z** items and **a** to **z** finance ratios,.

*Why finance experts and most of the people trapped in T-account formats?* Because they never know any other method, to makes Paccioli's financial reports easier. They need experts in better communication and visuals. Every body see the apple falls, only Newton see the gravity. OK?

*Will this new methods widely spread?* People want better finance understanding! Let the best method wins!!

*Will there be many sabotage?* Sure, it's hard to shift from old paradigm. Especially if the new one, make ruling class loose the monopoly. Even *Socrates* get poisoned![203]

The real corporate money invested is the sales or revenue (**S**) for its real wealth or asset utilized (**W**), so then (**S/W**) is the first important liquidity ratio for the business.

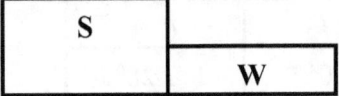

Total liability (**L**) in general is covered by debtor's wealth or total assets (**W**), so (**L/W**) is its coverage portion

W | L

As part of the liabilities (**L**), some xpress debt must be paid soon (**X**), so (**X/L**)= be an important liquidity ratio.

L | X

A part of xpress debt (**X**), unavoidable used for zero trade items (**Z**), so (**Z/X**) be the corporate's weakness ratio.

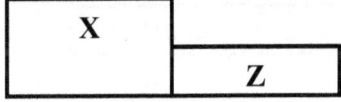

Using permutations and combinations of our **A** to **Z**, *IFRS* standard, we can create as many finance ratio as neded= 26!+25!+24!+… +2!= 650+600+552+… +2=**5,850**. finance ratios possible. It is hundred times more varied of the thickest financial analysis book known today! We know the financial ratio possibilities, much better than others!!

# Finance *Neuschwanstein*[205] Architecture of BMW

Please look at visuals af pages **147-159**, to show how we build finance architecture construction of BMW Incorporated We can also apply the ideas to any formats.

|   | 2010 | 2009 | (+) | (%) |
|---|---|---|---|---|
| c | 140.00% | 65.95% | 74.05% | 112.28% |
| d | 20.00% | 2.48% | 17.52% | 708.00% |
| f | 10.00% | 12.36% | -2.36% | -19.12% |
| g | 45.00 | 17.05 | 27.95 | 163.88% |
| i | 2.00% | 0.00% | 2.00% | #DIV/0! |
| j | 10.00 | 6.54 | 3.46 | 52.90% |
| l | 100.00% | 360.35% | -260.35% | -72.25% |
| p | 24.00 | 28.86 | (4.86) | -16.85% |
| q | 100.00% | 34.56% | 65.44% | 189.32% |
| s | 10.00% | -14.29% | 24.29% | -169.97% |
| t | 30.00% | 66.61% | -36.61% | -54.96% |
| v | 80.00% | 86.04% | -6.04% | -7.02% |
| y | 30.00% | 0.00% | 30.00% | #DIV/0! |

By the end of 2010, BMW can have 10% sales or revenue growth (**s**). We know that its previous sales or revenue (**S'**)=37,980 or growing (**s'**)= -14.29% from its two years ago **S"**=44,313. So it is realistic and no big deal, **S**=(1+**s**)**S'** =(1+10%) x 37,980= 41,778. *Just like that!*

Then we follow the key-piles and lock-stone ratios to complete all it's **A** to **Z** finance items and **a** to **z** ratios.

# BMW Accounting *Hohenschwangau*[206] Architecture

If it needs variable portion (**v**)=80%, its variable xpenses (**V**)=**Sv**=41,778x80%=33,422. So then margin of contribution (**M**)= (**S-V**)=41,778-33,422=8,356.

| 41,778 | 33,422 | | | | | |
|---|---|---|---|---|---|---|
| latest | 8,356 | 4,178 | | | | |
| | | 4,178 | 836 | | | |
| | | | 3,342 | 1,003 | | |
| | | | | 2,340 | 468 | 140 |
| previous | | | | | | 328 |
| 37,980 | | | | | 1,872 | |

**BMW-10**

| 4,410 | 7,799 | 14,451 | 7,226 | 5,570 | 4,178 |
|---|---|---|---|---|---|
| 1,161 | | | | | 1,393 |
| 2,228 | | | | 1,655 | |
| | 6,653 | | 7,226 | 5,354 | |
| | | | | 1,872 | |

If it needs fixed portion (**f**)=10%, its fixed xpenses (**F**)=**Sf**=41,778x10%=5,189. So then its operational surplus (**O**)= (**M-F**)=10,379-4,178=4,178.

If it also needs investment or financial portion (**i**)=2%, its investment or financial xpenses (**I**)=**Si**= 41,778x2%=836. So then its before tax income (**B**)= (**O-I**)= 4,178-836=3,342. *It's Paccioli's rule.*

We just translating it the visual finance architecture, geometric and algebra form, to make it better understood.

If it needs tax rate (**t**)=30%, its tax paid (**T**)= **Bt**= 3,342x30%=1,003. So then its after tax income (**A**)= (**B-T**)= 3,342-1,003=2,340.

|   | 2010 | 2009 | (+) | (%) |
|---|------|------|-----|-----|
| a | 16.19% | 0.82% | 15.37% | 1875.34% |
| b | 23.13% | 2.45% | 20.67% | 842.19% |
| e | 25.90% | 3.68% | 22.22% | 603.98% |
| h | 6.12% | 0.00% | 6.12% | #DIV/0! |
| k | 79.17% | 26.30% | 52.87% | 201.05% |
| m | 289.09% | 154.10% | 135.00% | 87.61% |
| n | 4.48% | 0.52% | 3.96% | 763.71% |
| o | 28.91% | 2.45% | 26.45% | 1077.74% |
| r | 12.95% | 0.80% | 12.15% | 1520.38% |
| u | 34.96% | 3.82% | 31.14% | 815.12% |
| w | 11.00 | (18.35) | 29.35 | -159.95% |
| x | 77.09% | 43.26% | 33.83% | 78.19% |
| z | 19.27% | 35.24% | -15.97% | -45.31% |

If it also needs dividend payout rate (**d**)=20%, its dividend paid (**D**)=**Ad**=2,340x20%=468. So then its retained earnings (**R**)= (**A-D**)=2,340-468=1,872.

If it also needs yielding tax of dividend (**y**)=30%, its yielding tax paid (**Y**)=**Dy**=468x30%=140. So then its home taken dividend (**H**)= (**D-Y**)=468-140=328.

They are very simple for Income Statement items.

# *Alpenvorland*[208] **of BMW Accounting**

Now, let's try its Balanche-sheet items. Its utilized capital at the beginning (**U**) is the equity at the end of the previous year (**E'**), so then (**U=E'**), then **E=(U+R)=** 5,354+1,872=7,226. It's still follow *Paccioli's rule.*

|   | 2010 | 2009 | (+) | (%) |
|---|---|---|---|---|
| A | 2,340 | 202 | 2,138 | 1058.20% |
| B | 3,342 | 605 | 2,737 | 452.44% |
| C | 7,799 | 5,505 | 2,294 | 41.66% |
| D | 468 | 5 | 463 | 9258.27% |
| E | 7,226 | 5,354 | 1,872 | 34.96% |
| F | 4,178 | 4,696 | (518) | -11.03% |
| G | 4,178 | 1,548 | 2,630 | 169.88% |
| H | 328 | - | 328 | #DIV/0! |
| I | 836 | - | 836 | #DIV/0! |
| J | 2,228 | 690 | 1,538 | 222.92% |
| K | 1,161 | 2,195 | (1,035) | -47.13% |
| L | 7,226 | 19,293 | (12,067) | -62.55% |
| M | 8,356 | 5,301 | 3,055 | 57.62% |

If it needs better stability, its leverage or gearing ratio (**l**)=100%, its liability at the total (**L**)=**El**=7,226x 100%=7,226. So then its wealth or total asset (**W**)= (**E+L**)=7,226+7,226=14,471.

Aimed procured inventory days (**p**)=24, its procured inventory (**P**)=(**Vp**/360)=33,422x24/360=2,228.

# BMW Finance's *Naturwissenschaft*[209] Architecture

Let's deal with the current ratio $(c)=(C/X)=120\%$ and quick or acid test ratio $(q)=(C-P)/X=100\%$ concepts.

|   | 2010 | 2009 | (+) | (%) |
|---|------|------|-----|-----|
| N | 6,653 | 19,142 | (12,489) | -65.25% |
| O | 4,178 | 605 | 3,573 | 590.55% |
| P | 2,228 | 2,620 | (392) | -14.96% |
| Q | 1,655 | 10,946 | (9,291) | -84.88% |
| R | 1,872 | 197 | 1,675 | 850.08% |
| S | 41,778 | 37,980 | 3,798 | 10.00% |
| T | 1,003 | 403 | 600 | 148.80% |
| U | 5,354 | 5,157 | 197 | 3.82% |
| V | 33,422 | 32,679 | 743 | 2.27% |
| W | 14,451 | 24,647 | (10,196) | -41.37% |
| X | 5,570 | 8,347 | (2,777) | -33.26% |
| Y | 140 | - | 140 | #DIV/0! |
| Z | 1,393 | 6,799 | (5,406) | -79.52% |

Since $c=(C/X)$ then $C=Xc$ and since $q=(C-P)/X$, then $(C-P)=Xq$ or $C=Xq+P$. It means that $(C=C)$ or $Xc=Xq+P$, so $(Xc-Xq)=P$ or $X(c-q)=P$, then $X=P/(c-q)=2,228/(140\%-100\%)=(2,228/40\%)=5,570$.

So, $C=Xc=5,570\times140\%=7,799$ and the quoted long-term debt $(Q)=(L-X)=7,226-5,570=1,655$. If it needs good or trade account payable days $(g)=45$, its good payable $(G)=(Vg/360)=33,422\times45/360=4,178$.

# Accounting *Residenz*[210] of BMW Architecture

So then its zero trade related xpress debt that must be paid quickly $(Z)= (X-G)=5,570-4,178=1,393.$

| | | | | | | |
|---|---|---|---|---|---|---|
| 37,980 | 32,679 | | | | | |
| latest | 5,301 | 4,696 | | | | |
| | | 605 | - | | | |
| | | | 605 | 403 | | |
| | | | | 202 | 5 | - |
| previous | | | | | | - |
| 44,313 | | | | 197 | | |

**BMW-09**

| | | | | | |
|---|---|---|---|---|---|
| 2,195 | 5,505 | 24,647 | 19,293 | 8,347 | 1,548 |
| 690 | | | | | 6,799 |
| 2,620 | | | | 10,946 | |
| | 19,142 | | 5,354 | 5,157 | |
| | | | | 197 | |

If it also needs job trade account receivable days $(j)=10$, its job trade account receivables $(J)=(Sj/360)=41,778\times10/360=1,161.$ So then its kind of cash $(K)= (C-J-P)=7,799-1,161-2,228=4,410.$ *It's a conservative one.*

So then its total non current, fix and intangible assets $(N)= (W-C)=14,451-7,799=6,653.$

Mission accomplished, the finance algebra has identified all **A** to **Z** financial architecture items, coherence with *IFRS* standards, and finance architecture made easy. Is it easier? Hopefullu those help you understand it better.

We shall analyze this suggested BMW finance architecture blue-print! Not necessary, but we prove them!

| 44,313 | 37,833 | | | | | |
|---|---|---|---|---|---|---|
| latest | 6,480 | 6,085 | | | | |
| | | 395 | - | | | |
| | | | 395 | 11 | | |
| | | | | 384 | 187 | - |
| previous | | | | | | - |
| - | | | | | 197 | |

**BMW-08**

| 3,970 | 7,538 | 23,316 | 17,978 | 7,974 | 1,276 |
|---|---|---|---|---|---|
| 982 | | | | | 6,698 |
| 2,586 | | | | 10,004 | |
| | 15,778 | | 5,338 | 5,141 | |
| | | | | 197 | |

The-26 **IFRS'** (*International Finance Reporting Standard*'s) ratios consist of 13 financial architecture key-piles[33] and 13 others locked-stones[34]. The-13 key-piles are:

01: **c**= Current ratio= (**C/X**)=7,799/5,570=**140.00%**

02: **d**= Dividend paid portion to after tax= (**D/A**)= 468/2,340= **20.00%**, *it's sharp!!*

03: **f**= Fix expenses portion to revenue= (**F/S**)= 4,178/41,778= **10.00%**, *it's sharp!!*

04: **g**= Goods or trade account payable days= (360**G/V**)= 360x4,178/33,422=**45.00**, *it's sharp!!*

05: **i**= Investment or financial portion to revenue= (**I/S**)=
836/41,778=**2.00%**, *it's sharp!!*

06: **j**= Job or trade account receivable days= (360**J/S**)=
360x1,161/33,422=**10.00**, *it's sharp!!*

|   | 2009 | 2008 | (+) | (%) |
|---|---|---|---|---|
| c | 65.95% | 94.53% | -28.58% | -30.23% |
| d | 2.48% | 48.70% | -46.22% | -94.92% |
| f | 12.36% | 13.73% | -1.37% | -9.96% |
| g | 17.05 | 12.14 | 4.91 | 40.45% |
| i | 0.00% | 0.00% | 0.00% | #DIV/0! |
| j | 6.54 | 7.98 | (1.44) | -18.02% |
| l | 360.35% | 336.79% | 23.55% | 6.99% |
| p | 28.86 | 24.61 | 4.26 | 17.29% |
| q | 34.56% | 62.10% | -27.54% | -44.34% |
| s | -14.29% | | | |
| t | 66.61% | 2.78% | 63.83% | 2291.96% |
| v | 86.04% | 85.38% | 0.67% | 0.78% |
| y | 0.00% | 0.00% | 0.00% | #DIV/0! |

07: **l**= Leverage or gearing = debt equity ratio= *DER*=
(**L/E**)=7,226/7,226=**100.00%,** *it's sharp!!*

08: **p**= Procurred inventory days= (360**P/V**)=360x2,228
/33,422=**24.00**, *it's sharp!!*

09: **q**= Quick or acid test ratio= (**C-P**)/**X**=(7,799-2,228)
/5,570=**100.00%,** *it's sharp!!*

# BMW Finance *Karwendelgebirge*[213] Architecture

10: **s**= Sales or revenue growth to previous= $(S/S'-1)$= 41,778/37,980-1=**10.00%**, *it's sharp!!*

|   | 2009 | 2008 | (+) | (%) |
|---|------|------|-----|-----|
| a | 0.82% | 1.65% | -0.83% | -50.24% |
| b | 2.45% | 1.69% | 0.76% | 44.89% |
| e | 3.68% | 3.69% | -0.01% | -0.30% |
| h | 0.00% | 0.00% | 0.00% | #DIV/0! |
| k | 26.30% | 49.79% | -23.49% | -47.18% |
| m | 154.10% | 190.05% | -35.96% | -18.92% |
| n | 0.52% | 0.44% | 0.07% | 16.67% |
| o | 2.45% | 1.69% | 0.76% | 44.89% |
| r | 0.80% | 0.84% | -0.05% | -5.40% |
| u | 3.82% | 3.83% | -0.01% | -0.31% |
| w | (18.35) | (20.44) | 2.09 | -10.24% |
| x | 43.26% | 44.35% | -1.09% | -2.46% |
| z | 35.24% | 37.26% | -2.02% | -5.41% |

11: **t**= Tax rate or portion to before tax earnings= $(T/B)$= 1,003/3,342=**30.00%**, *it's sharp!!*

12: **v**= Variable expenses portion to revenue= $(V/S)$= 33,422/41,778=**80.00%**, *it's sharp!!*

13: **y**= Yielding tax of the dividend paid= $(Y/D)$=140 /468= **30.00%**, *it's sharp!!*

　　　All 13 (thirteen) *key-pile* finance architecture ratios can be set sharp, and guaranteed to perform accurately sharp

# Accounting *Olympic Tent*[214] of BMW

The 13 (thirteen) *locked-stone* finance architecture ratios just a derivative of its *key-piles* ratio and not sharp.

|   | 2009 | 2008 | (+) | (%) |
|---|------|------|-----|-----|
| A | 202 | 384 | (182) | -47.40% |
| B | 605 | 395 | 210 | 53.16% |
| C | 5,505 | 7,538 | (2,033) | -26.97% |
| D | 5.00 | 187.00 | (182) | -97.33% |
| E | 5,354 | 5,338 | 16 | 0.30% |
| F | 4,696 | 6,085 | (1,389) | -22.83% |
| G | 1,548 | 1,276 | 272 | 21.32% |
| H | - | - | - | #DIV/0! |
| I | - | - | - | #DIV/0! |
| J | 690 | 982 | (292) | -29.74% |
| K | 2,195 | 3,970 | (1,775) | -44.71% |
| L | 19,293 | 17,978 | 1,315 | 7.31% |
| M | 5,301 | 6,480 | (1,179) | -18.19% |

01: **a**= After tax return on asset= **(A/W)**=2,340/14,451 =**16.19%**

02: **b**= Before tax return on asset= **(B/W)**=3,342/14,451 =**23.13%**

03: **e**= Equity return= return on equity= *ROE*= **(R/E)**= 1,872 /7,226=**25.90%**

04: **h**= Home taken dividend to utilized equity= **(H/U)**= 328/5,354=**6.12%**

# BMW *Hauptbahnhof*[215] Finance Architecture

05. **k**= Kind of cash liquidity ratio= **(K/X)**=4,410/5,570
 =**79.17%**

|   | 2009 | 2008 | (+) | (%) |
|---|---|---|---|---|
| N | 19,142 | 15,778 | 3,364 | 21.32% |
| O | 605 | 395 | 210 | 53.16% |
| P | 2,620 | 2,586 | 34 | 1.31% |
| Q | 10,946 | 10,004 | 942 | 9.42% |
| R | 197 | 197 | - | 0.00% |
| S | 37,980 | 44,313 | (6,333) | -14.29% |
| T | 403 | 11 | 392 | 3563.64% |
| U | 5,157 | 5,141 | 16 | 0.31% |
| V | 32,679 | 37,833 | (5,154) | -13.62% |
| W | 24,647 | 23,316 | 1,331 | 5.71% |
| X | 8,347 | 7,974 | 373 | 4.68% |
| Y | - | - | - | #DIV/0! |
| Z | 6,799 | 6,698 | 101 | 1.51% |

06. **m**= Market-run or asset turn-over= *ATO*= **(S/W)**=
 41,778/14,451=**289.09%**
07. **n**= NPM= net profit margin= **(R/S)**=1,872/41,778
 =**4.48%**
08. **o**= Operational surplus to asset return= **(O/W)**=4,178
 /14,451=**28.51%**
09. **r**= Return of net earnings on assets= *ROA*= **(R/W)**=
 1,872/14,451=**12.95%**

# BMW *Nuremberg*[216] Accounting Architecture

The remaining 4 (four) locked-stone finance architecture ratios are as follow:

10: **u**= Utilized return on starting equity= (**R/U**)= 1,872 /5,354=**34.96%**

11: **w**= Working capital days required= (**g-p-j**)= 45.00-24.00-10.00=**11.00**, *supplier financed!*

12: **x**= Xpress or current to total debt portion= (**X/L**)= 5,570/7,226=**77.89%**

13: **z**= Zero trade liability portion of total debts= (**Z/L**)= 1,393/7,226= **19.27%**

*Will this finance architecture change the present accounting?* Not necessary. This only change the finance analysis and sysnthesis, not impacting the accounting recordsg. As we prove before, finance architecture could work with any accounting system, with same benefits.

*Does alignment in accounting helps making finance architecture better?* Sure, even though did not required, a coherence synchronization will support it to perform better.

*What are the differences between finance and accounting?* Accounting starts from evidences, making tickets, entries and completed with financial reports. On the other hand, finance starts from financial reaports and ends with financial analysis, supporting and advising actions.

*Does finance architecture help its analysis?* Not just analysis, it also help the synthesis, so we can make and assure good finance performance in the relevant future.

*Will that be any limitation stops it?* Inconsistency, could be the reason why the knowledgeable people fails.

*Could finance architecture ensure the desired target achievement?* Sure, it prepares future finance architecture blue-print, that will perform if *followed well consistently*.

## CHAPTER-XIII: Finance Architecture Variants

One of the main problem in corporate finance is using other people's money in its operations, or working capital management for its variable or cost of goods (**V**).

Corporate normally get the supplier's money as good or trade account payables (**g**) at goods payable days, **g**=(360G/V), as sources of free short-term corporate funds.

So then it can stored at procured inventory (**P**) for procured inventory days, **p**=(360P/V). It also give job account receivables (**J**) at job receivable days, **j**=(360J/S). The two (**p+j**) then condered as short-term funds usages.

| j | g |
|---|---|
| p |   |
|   | W |

Corporate working capital, **w**=(**g-p-j**), just short-term sources and its usages. If positive means it gains other people's money and if negative means it must finance them by itself to make the business run. Just try to get it positive!

| C | X |
|---|---|
|   | Q |
| N |   |
|   | E |

The wisdom is get current assts ( **C**) greater then xpress debts (**X**), by utiulizing quoted long-term debts (**Q**), then maintain the rest as non current assets (**N**). Equity, **E**=(**C+N**)-(**X+Q**) as stated in British financial statements, be the net wealth from all sources and uses of funds.

# Finance *Nava l* [217] **Architecture of Mitsubish***i*

Please look at visuals af pages **160-172**, to show how we build finance architecture construction of Mitsubishi Inc We can also apply the ideas to any formats.

|   | 2010 | 2009 | (+) | (%) |
|---|---|---|---|---|
| c | 150.00% | 43.44% | 106.56% | 245.32% |
| d | 40.00% | 34.79% | 5.21% | 14.96% |
| f | 10.00% | 14.46% | -4.46% | -30.83% |
| g | 80.00 | 78.75 | 1.25 | 1.59% |
| i | 2.00% | 0.93% | 1.07% | 115.76% |
| j | 24.00 | 30.23 | (6.23) | -20.61% |
| l | 100.00% | 288.48% | -188.48% | -65.34% |
| p | 45.00 | 54.63 | (9.63) | -17.63% |
| q | 100.00% | 19.66% | 80.34% | 408.64% |
| s | 10.00% | -26.75% | 36.75% | -137.38% |
| t | 30.00% | 37.01% | -7.01% | -18.95% |
| v | 80.00% | 83.81% | -3.81% | -4.55% |
| y | 30.00% | 0.00% | 30.00% | #DIV/0! |

By the end of 2010, Mitsubishi can have 10% sales or revenue growth (**s**). We know that its previous sales or revenue (**S'**)=1,446 or growing (**s'**)= -26.75% from its two years ago **S"**=1,974. So it is realistic and no big deal, **S**=(1+**s**)**S'** =(1+10%) x1,446= 1,590. *Just like that!*

Then we follow the key-piles and lock-stone ratios to complete all it's **A** to **Z** finance items and **a** to **z** ratios.

# Mitsubishi Accounting *Aircraft*[218] Architecture

If it needs variable portion (**v**)=80%, its variable xpenses (**V**)=Sv=1,590x80%=1,272. So then margin of contribution (**M**)= (**S-V**)=1,590-1,272=318.

| 1,590 | 1,272 | | | | | |
|---|---|---|---|---|---|---|
| latest | 318 | 159 | | | | |
| | | 159 | 32 | | | |
| | | | 127 | 38 | | |
| | | | | 89 | 36 | 11 |
| previous | | | | | | 25 |
| 1,446 | | | | | 53 | |

**Mitsubishi-10**

| 212 | 477 | 755 | 377 | 318 | 283 |
|---|---|---|---|---|---|
| 106 | | | | | 35 |
| 159 | | | | 59 | |
| | 278 | | 377 | 324 | |
| | | | | 53 | |

If it needs fixed portion (**f**)=10%, its fixed xpenses (**F**)=Sf=1,590x10%=159. So then its operational surplus (**O**)= (**M-F**)=318-159=159.

If it also needs investment or financial portion (**i**)=2%, its investment or financial xpenses (**I**)=Si= 1,590x2%=32. So then its before tax income (**B**)= (**O-I**)= 159-32=127. *It's Paccioli's rule.*

We just translating it the visual finance architecture, geometric and algebra form, to make it better understood.

# *Atomic Farm*[219] **Finance Architecture at Mitsubishi**

If it needs tax rate $(t)$=30%, its tax paid $(T)$= $Bt$= 127x30%=38. So then its after tax income $(A)$= $(B-T)$= 127-38=89.

|   | 2010 | 2009 | (+) | (%) |
|---|---|---|---|---|
| a | 11.80% | 0.58% | 11.22% | 1934.03% |
| b | 16.85% | 0.92% | 15.93% | 1730.20% |
| e | 14.16% | 1.47% | 12.69% | 863.58% |
| h | 7.70% | 0.00% | 7.70% | #DIV/0! |
| k | 66.67% | 3.96% | 62.70% | 1582.51% |
| m | 210.66% | 114.85% | 95.81% | 83.42% |
| n | 3.36% | 0.33% | 3.03% | 920.44% |
| o | 21.07% | 1.99% | 19.08% | 961.03% |
| r | 7.08% | 0.38% | 6.70% | 1771.65% |
| u | 16.49% | 1.49% | 15.00% | 1005.99% |
| w | 11.00 | (6.12) | 17.12 | -279.87% |
| x | 84.26% | 82.73% | 1.53% | 1.85% |
| z | 9.36% | 54.38% | -45.01% | -82.78% |

If it also needs dividend payout rate $(d)$=40%, its dividend paid $(D)$=$Ad$=89x40%=36. So then its retained earnings $(R)$= $(A-D)$=89-36=53.

If it also needs yielding tax of dividend $(y)$=30%, its yielding tax paid $(Y)$=$Dy$=36x30%=11. So then its home taken dividend $(H)$= $(D-Y)$=36-11=25.

They are very simple for Income Statement items.

# *Power Supply*[220] **Architecture of Mitsubishi Finance**

Now, let's try its Balanche-sheet items. Its utilized capital at the beginning (**U**) is the equity at the end of the previous year (**E'**), so then (**U=E'**), then **E**=(**U+R**)= 324+53=377. It's still follow *Paccioli's rule*.

|   | 2010 | 2009 | (+) | (%) |
|---|------|------|-----|-----|
| A | 89 | 7 | 82 | 1119.87% |
| B | 127 | 12 | 116 | 997.62% |
| C | 477 | 336 | 141 | 42.02% |
| D | 36 | 3 | 33 | 1302.37% |
| E | 377 | 324 | 53 | 16.49% |
| F | 159 | 209 | (50) | -23.91% |
| G | 283 | 265 | 18 | 6.67% |
| H | 25 | - | 25 | #DIV/0! |
| I | 32 | 13 | 18 | 137.34% |
| J | 159 | 121 | 38 | 31.00% |
| K | 106 | 31 | 75 | 245.99% |
| L | 377 | 935 | (557) | -59.62% |
| M | 318 | 234 | 84 | 35.92% |

If it needs better stability, its leverage or gearing ratio (**I**)=100%, its liability at the total (**L**)=**EI**=377x 100%=377. So then its wealth or total asset (**W**)= (**E+L**)=377+377=755.

Aimed procured inventory days (**p**)=45, its procured inventory (**P**)=(**Vp**/360)=1,272x45/360=159.

Let's deal with the current ratio $(c)=(C/X)=150\%$ and quick or acid test ratio $(q)=(C-P)/X=100\%$ concepts.

|   | 2010 | 2009 | (+) | (%) |
|---|---|---|---|---|
| N | 278 | 923 | (645) | -69.89% |
| O | 159 | 25 | 134 | 536.33% |
| P | 159 | 184 | (25) | -13.52% |
| Q | 59 | 161 | (102) | -63.20% |
| R | 53 | 5 | 49 | 1022.48% |
| S | 1,590 | 1,446 | 145 | 10.00% |
| T | 38 | 4 | 34 | 789.61% |
| U | 324 | 319 | 5 | 1.49% |
| V | 1,272 | 1,212 | 61 | 4.99% |
| W | 755 | 1,259 | (504) | -40.03% |
| X | 318 | 773 | (455) | -58.87% |
| Y | 11 | - | 11 | #DIV/0! |
| Z | 35 | 508 | (473) | -93.05% |

Since $c=(C/X)$ then $C=Xc$ and since $q=(C-P)/X$, then $(C-P)=Xq$ or $C=Xq+P$. It means that $(C=C)$ or $Xc=Xq+P$, so $(Xc-Xq)=P$ or $X(c-q)=P$, then $X=P/(c-q)=159/(150\%-100\%)=(159/50\%)=318$.

So, $C=Xc=318\times150\%=477$ and the quoted long-term debt $(Q)=(L-X)=377-318=59$. If it needs good or trade account payable  days $(g)=80$, its good payable $(G)=(Vg/360)=1,272\times80/360=283$.

So then its zero trade related xpress debt that must be paid quickly $(\mathbf{Z})= (\mathbf{X\text{-}G})=318\text{-}283=35$.

| 1,446 | 1,212 | | | | | |
|---|---|---|---|---|---|---|
| latest | 234 | 209 | | | | |
| | | 25 | 13 | | | |
| | | | 12 | 4 | | |
| | | | | 7 | 3 | - |
| previous | | | | | | - |
| 1,974 | | | | | 5 | |

**Mitsubishi-09**

| 31 | 336 | 1,259 | 935 | 773 | 265 |
|---|---|---|---|---|---|
| 121 | | | | | 508 |
| 184 | | | | 161 | |
| | 923 | | 324 | 319 | |
| | | | | 5 | |

If it also needs job trade account receivable days $(\mathbf{j})=24$, its job trade account receivables $(\mathbf{J})=(\mathbf{Sj}/360)= 1,590\text{x}24/360=106$. So then its kind of cash $(\mathbf{K})= (\mathbf{C\text{-}J\text{-}P})=477\text{-}106\text{-}159=212$. *It's a conservative one.*

So then its total non current, fix and intangible assets $(\mathbf{N})= (\mathbf{W\text{-}C})=755\text{-}477=278$.

Mission accomplished, the finance algebra has identified all **A** to **Z** financial architecture items, coherence with **IFRS** standards, and finance architecture made easy. Is it easier? Hopefullu those help you understand it better.

# Mitsubishi *Taisho*[223] Finance Architecture

We shall analyze this suggested Mitsubishi finance architecture blue-print! Not necessary, but we prove them!

| 1,974 | 1,663 | | | | | |
|---|---|---|---|---|---|---|
| latest | 310 | 242 | | | | |
| | | 68 | 15 | | | |
| | | | 54 | 1 | | |
| | | | | 53 | 107 | - |
| previous | | | | | | - |
| - | | | | (55) | | |

**Mitsubishi-08**

| 31 | 310 | 1,138 | 819 | 620 | 156 |
|---|---|---|---|---|---|
| 90 | | | | | 464 |
| 189 | | | | 199 | |
| | 828 | | 319 | 374 | |
| | | | | (55) | |

The-26 *IFRS*' (*International Finance Reporting Standard*'s) ratios consist of 13 financial architecture key-piles[33] and 13 others locked-stones[34]. The-13 key-piles are:

01: **c**= Current ratio= **(C/X)**=477/318=**150.00%**

02: **d**= Dividend paid portion to after tax= **(D/A)**= 36/89= **40.00%**, *it's sharp!!*

03: **f**= Fix expenses portion to revenue= **(F/S)**= 159 /1590= **10.00%**, *it's sharp!!*

04: **g**= Goods or trade account payable days= (360**G/V**)= 360x283/1,272=**80.00**, *it's sharp!!*

# _Showa_[224] for Mitsubishi Accounting Architecture

05: **i**= Investment or financial portion to revenue= (**I/S**)=
  32/1,590=**2.00%**, _it's sharp!!_

06: **j**= Job or trade account receivable days= (360**J/S**)=
  360x106/1,590=**24.00**, _it's sharp!!_

|   | 2009 | 2008 | (+) | (%) |
|---|------|------|-----|-----|
| c | 43.44% | 49.96% | -6.52% | -13.05% |
| d | 34.79% | 204.31% | -169.52% | -82.97% |
| f | 14.46% | 12.27% | 2.19% | 17.81% |
| g | 78.75 | 33.68 | 45.06 | 133.80% |
| i | 0.93% | 0.74% | 0.19% | 25.73% |
| j | 30.23 | 16.34 | 13.89 | 84.96% |
| l | 288.48% | 256.46% | 32.02% | 12.48% |
| p | 54.63 | 40.93 | 13.70 | 33.47% |
| q | 19.66% | 19.46% | 0.20% | 1.01% |
| s | -26.75% | | | |
| t | 37.01% | 2.07% | 34.95% | 1691.38% |
| v | 83.81% | 84.27% | -0.46% | -0.54% |
| y | 0.00% | 0.00% | 0.00% | #DIV/0! |

07: **l**= Leverage or gearing = debt equity ratio= _DER_=
  (**L/E**)=377/377=**100.00%**, _it's sharp!!_

08: **p**= Procurred inventory days= (360**P/V**)=360x159
  /1,272=**45.00**, _it's sharp!!_

09: **q**= Quick or acid test ratio= (**C-P**)/**X**=(477-159)
  /318=**100.00%**, _it's sharp!!_

# Mitsubishi Finance *Keiretsu*[225] Architecture

10: **s**= Sales or revenue growth to previous= **(S/S'-1)**= 1,590/1,446-1=**10.00%**, *it's sharp!!*

|   | 2009 | 2008 | (+) | (%) |
|---|---|---|---|---|
| a | 0.58% | 4.62% | -4.04% | -87.45% |
| b | 0.92% | 4.72% | -3.80% | -80.49% |
| e | 1.47% | -17.19% | 18.66% | -108.55% |
| h | 0.00% | 0.00% | 0.00% | #DIV/0! |
| k | 3.96% | 5.01% | -1.05% | -20.97% |
| m | 114.85% | 173.42% | -58.57% | -33.77% |
| n | 0.33% | -2.78% | 3.11% | -111.84% |
| o | 1.99% | 6.00% | -4.01% | -66.90% |
| r | 0.38% | -4.82% | 5.20% | -107.84% |
| u | 1.49% | -14.67% | 16.16% | -110.16% |
| w | (6.12) | (23.60) | 17.48 | -74.08% |
| x | 82.73% | 75.74% | 7.00% | 9.24% |
| z | 54.38% | 56.73% | -2.35% | -4.15% |

11: **t**= Tax rate or portion to before tax earnings= **(T/B)**= 38/127=**30.00%**, *it's sharp!!*
12: **v**= Variable expenses portion to revenue= **(V/S)**= 1,272/1590=**80.00%**, *it's sharp!!*
13: **y**= Yielding tax of the dividend paid= **(Y/D)**=11/25= **30.00%**, *it's sharp!!*

All 13 (thirteen) *key-pile* finance architecture ratios can be set sharp, and guaranted to perform accurately sharp

# Accounting *Polymer*[226] of Mitsubishi Architecture

The 13 (thirteen) *locked-stone* finance architecture ratios just a derivative of its *key-piles* ratio and not sharp.

|   | 2009 | 2008 | (+) | (%) |
|---|------|------|-----|-----|
| A | 7 | 53 | (45) | -86.12% |
| B | 12 | 54 | (42) | -78.43% |
| C | 336 | 310 | 26 | 8.43% |
| D | 2.54 | 107.49 | (105) | -97.64% |
| E | 324 | 319 | 5 | 1.49% |
| F | 209 | 242 | (33) | -13.70% |
| G | 265 | 156 | 109 | 70.33% |
| H | - | - | - | #DIV/0! |
| I | 13 | 15 | (1) | -7.90% |
| J | 121 | 90 | 32 | 35.48% |
| K | 31 | 31 | (0) | -1.45% |
| L | 935 | 819 | 116 | 14.16% |
| M | 234 | 310 | (76) | -24.63% |

01: **a**= After tax return on asset= (**A/W**)=89/755 =**11.80%**

02: **b**= Before tax return on asset= (**B/W**)=127/755 =**16.85%**

03: **e**= Equity return= return on equity= *ROE*= (**R/E**)= 53 /377=**14.16%**

04: **h**= Home taken dividend to utilized equity= (**H/U**)= 25/324=**7.70%**

# Mitsubishi *Kaigun*[227] Finance Architecture

05. **k**= Kind of cash liquidity ratio= (**K/X**)=212/318
=**66.67%**

|   | 2009 | 2008 | (+) | (%) |
|---|------|------|-----|-----|
| N | 923 | 828 | 95 | 11.42% |
| O | 25 | 68 | (43) | -63.40% |
| P | 184 | 189 | (5) | -2.77% |
| Q | 161 | 199 | (37) | -18.76% |
| R | 5 | (55) | 60 | -108.67% |
| S | 1,446 | 1,974 | (528) | -26.75% |
| T | 4 | 1 | 3 | 286.49% |
| U | 319 | 374 | (55) | -14.67% |
| V | 1,212 | 1,663 | (451) | -27.15% |
| W | 1,259 | 1,138 | 121 | 10.60% |
| X | 773 | 620 | 153 | 24.70% |
| Y | - | - | - | #DIV/0! |
| Z | 508 | 464 | 44 | 9.42% |

06. **m**= Market-run or asset turn-over= *ATO*= (**S/W**)=
1,590/755=**210.66%**
07. **n**= NPM= net profit margin= (**R/S**)=53/1,590 =**3.36%**
08. **o**= Operational surplus to asset return= (**O/W**)= 159
/755=**21.07%**
09. **r**= Return of net earnings on assets= *ROA*= (**R/W**)= 53
/755=**7.08%**

# <u>Sogososha[228]</u> Mitsubishi Accounting Architecture

The remaining 4 (four) locked-stone finance architecture ratios are as follow:

10: **u**= Utilized return on starting equity= (**R/U**)= 53 /324 =**16.49%**

11: **w**= Working capital days required= (**g-p-j**)=80.00-45.00-24.00=**11.00**, *supplier financed!*

12: **x**= Xpress or current to total debt portion= (**X/L**)= 318 /377=**84.26%**

13: **z**= Zero trade liability portion of total debts= (**Z/L**)= 35/377= **9.36%**

*Have we find some thing new with finacnce architecture so far?* Yes, now we know that (**R/U**)=**R**/(**E-R**) is a better and more realistic investment profitability measures than what commonly known as *ROE*= *return on equity* at the end= (**R/E**). Better on **U** as its starting equity.

*Why in hudred of years not so many people see that mistakes?* Two reasons. <u>First</u>, common people too confused with difficult finance setting at pass it to finance experts. <u>Second</u>, finance experts learn it hard as unquestionalble sacred cow, and miss the common senses on its measures.

*Why that problem definition in finance architecture commonly missed?* It's a logical inconsistendy. All people live in building for many years, and know it very well, but still assign architects to make it an optimum architecture.

*What happen if there is no architect?* Brick-layers and carpenter, on even themselves can make the building, but not exactly at best money, technology or art possible.

*Does same thing happen in finance architecture?* <u>Exactly</u>, but even more serious than that because money is the most important thing on earth. It could be a *disaster*!

## CHAPTER-XIV: Regional Finance Architecture

Whether we like it or not, money had been the most important thing on earth. Its' te essence of all economic theories of exchange, business and welfare. So, the kind of cash (**K**), must be managed well in finance architecture.

People can get other people's money for free at the goods or trade account payables (**G**), so then (**K/G**) be the first important liquidity ratio for the business.

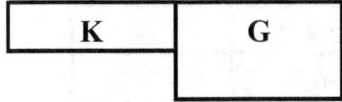

The **K** also covering its xpress liability (**X**), that must be paid soon, even though some part of it did not used for trade account payables, but the (**K/X**) is its total liquid portion for paying its xpress debts.

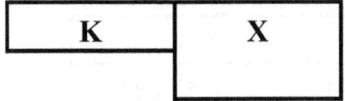

Greater than just **X**, its total liabilities or debts (**L**), can also covered by **K**, so (**Z/X**) be its fast liquidity ratio.

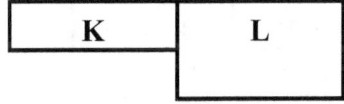

Proper understanding of finance architecture makes corporate finance a useful and valuable building, which is much better than just a self made house. It does not mean than the finance expert are stupid, but with proper finance arhitecture tool they'll be much more efficient. It's like a hammer help nails sticked better, than a bare hand. *Wow!*

# Finance *Ryoanji*[229] Architecture of Mitsui

Please look at visuals af pages **174-185**, to show how we build finance architecture construction of Mitsui Incorporated We can also apply the ideas to any formats.

|   | 2010 | 2009 | (+) | (%) |
|---|------|------|-----|-----|
| c | 120.00% | 167.77% | -47.77% | -28.47% |
| d | 20.00% | -306.60% | 326.60% | -106.52% |
| f | 10.00% | 12.93% | -2.93% | -22.64% |
| g | 180.00 | 163.23 | 16.77 | 10.27% |
| i | 2.00% | 1.13% | 0.87% | 76.77% |
| j | 120.00 | 163.36 | (43.36) | -26.54% |
| l | 100.00% | 275.27% | -175.27% | -63.67% |
| p | 45.00 | 53.54 | (8.54) | -15.95% |
| q | 100.00% | 146.56% | -46.56% | -31.77% |
| s | 5.00% | -21.34% | 26.34% | -123.43% |
| t | 30.00% | 70.79% | -40.79% | -57.62% |
| v | 75.00% | 82.86% | -7.86% | -9.49% |
| y | 30.00% | 0.00% | 30.00% | #DIV/0! |

By the end of 2010, BMW can have 5% sales or revenue growth (**s**). We know that its previous sales or revenue (**S'**)=43,840 or growing (**s'**)= -21.34% from its two years ago **S"**=55,733. So it is realistic and no big deal, **S**=(1+**s**)**S'** =(1+5%) x 43,840= 46,032. *Just like that!*

Then we follow the key-piles and lock-stone ratios to complete all it's **A** to **Z** finance items and **a** to **z** ratios.

# Mitsui Accounting *Todaiji*[230] Architecture

If it needs variable portion (**v**)=75%, its variable xpenses (**V**)=**Sv**=46,032x75%=34,524. So then margin of contribution (**M**)= (**S-V**)=46,032-34,524=11,508.

| | | | | | | |
|---|---|---|---|---|---|---|
| 46,032 | 34,524 | | | | | |
| latest | 11,508 | 4,603 | | | | |
| | | 6,905 | 921 | | | |
| | | | 5,984 | 1,795 | | |
| | | | | 4,189 | 838 | 251 |
| previous | | | | | | 586 |
| 43,840 | | | | | 3,351 | |

**Mitsui-10**

| | | | | | |
|---|---|---|---|---|---|
| 6,234 | 25,893 | 54,436 | 27,218 | 21,578 | 17,262 |
| 15,344 | | | | | 4,316 |
| 4,316 | | | | 5,641 | |
| | 28,543 | | 27,218 | 23,867 | |
| | | | | 3,351 | |

If it needs fixed portion (**f**)=10%, its fixed xpenses (**F**)=**Sf**=46,032x10%=4,603. So then its operational surplus (**O**)= (**M-F**)=11,508-4,603=6,905.

If it also needs investment or financial portion (**i**)=2%, its investment or financial xpenses (**I**)=**Si**= 46,032x2%=921. So then its before tax income (**B**)= (**O-I**)= 6,905-921=5,984. *It's Paccioli's rule.*

We just translating it the visual finance architecture, geometric and algebra form, to make it better understood.

## _Shorinji[231]_ Finance Architecture at Mitsui

If it needs tax rate (**t**)=30%, its tax paid (**T**)= **Bt**= 5,984x30%=1795. So then its after tax income (**A**)= (**B-T**)= 5,984-1,795=4,189.

|   | 2010 | 2009 | (+) | (%) |
|---|------|------|-----|-----|
| a | 7.70% | 0.44% | 7.26% | 1649.26% |
| b | 10.99% | 1.51% | 9.49% | 629.86% |
| e | 12.31% | 6.71% | 5.60% | 83.43% |
| h | 2.46% | 0.00% | 2.46% | #DIV/0! |
| k | 28.89% | 68.48% | -39.59% | -57.81% |
| m | 84.56% | 48.95% | 35.61% | 72.76% |
| n | 7.28% | 3.65% | 3.63% | 99.22% |
| o | 12.68% | 2.06% | 10.62% | 515.75% |
| r | 6.16% | 1.79% | 4.37% | 244.17% |
| u | 14.04% | 7.20% | 6.85% | 95.14% |
| w | 15.00 | (53.67) | 68.67 | -127.95% |
| x | 79.28% | 38.78% | 40.49% | 104.41% |
| z | 15.86% | 13.71% | 2.15% | 15.65% |

If it also needs dividend payout rate (**d**)=20%, its dividend paid (**D**)=**Ad**=4,189x20%=838. So then its retained earnings (**R**)= (**A-D**)=4,189-838=3,351.

If it also needs yielding tax of dividend (**y**)=30%, its yielding tax paid (**Y**)=**Dy**=838x30%=251. So then its home taken dividend (**H**)= (**D-Y**)=838-251=586.

They are very simple for Income Statement items.

# _Katsura_[232] **Architecture of Mitsui Accounting**

Now, let's try its Balanche-sheet items. Its utilized capital at the beginning (**U**) is the equity at the end of the previous year (**E'**), so then (**U=E'**), then **E=(U+R)**= 23,867+3,351=27,218. It's still follow _Paccioli's rule_.

|   | 2010 | 2009 | (+) | (%) |
|---|---|---|---|---|
| A | 4,189 | 394 | 3,795 | 963.18% |
| B | 5,984 | 1,349 | 4,635 | 343.60% |
| C | 25,893 | 42,745 | (16,852) | -39.42% |
| D | 838 | (1,208) | 2,046 | -169.35% |
| E | 27,218 | 23,867 | 3,351 | 14.04% |
| F | 4,603 | 5,667 | (1,064) | -18.77% |
| G | 17,262 | 16,472 | 790 | 4.80% |
| H | 586 | - | 586 | #DIV/0! |
| I | 921 | 496 | 425 | 85.61% |
| J | 4,316 | 19,894 | (15,579) | -78.31% |
| K | 15,344 | 17,448 | (2,104) | -12.06% |
| L | 27,218 | 65,698 | (38,480) | -58.57% |
| M | 11,508 | 7,512 | 3,996 | 53.19% |

If it needs better stability, its leverage or gearing ratio (**I**)=100%, its liability at the total (**L**)=**EI**=27,218x 100%=27,218. So then its wealth or total asset (**W**)= (**E+L**)=27,218+27,218=54,436.

Aimed procured inventory days (**p**)=45, its procured inventory (**P**)=(**Vp**/360)=34,524x45/360=4,316.

# Mitsui Finance's *Nara*[233] Architecture

Let's deal with the current ratio $(c)=(C/X)=120\%$ and quick or acid test ratio $(q)=(C-P)/X=100\%$ concepts.

|   | 2010 | 2009 | (+) | (%) |
|---|------|------|-----|-----|
| N | 28,543 | 46,820 | (18,277) | -39.04% |
| O | 6,905 | 1,845 | 5,060 | 274.24% |
| P | 4,316 | 5,403 | (1,088) | -20.13% |
| Q | 5,641 | 40,219 | (34,578) | -85.98% |
| R | 3,351 | 1,602 | 1,749 | 109.18% |
| S | 46,032 | 43,840 | 2,192 | 5.00% |
| T | 1,795 | 955 | 840 | 87.98% |
| U | 23,867 | 22,265 | 1,602 | 7.20% |
| V | 34,524 | 36,328 | (1,804) | -4.97% |
| W | 54,436 | 89,565 | (35,129) | -39.22% |
| X | 21,578 | 25,479 | (3,902) | -15.31% |
| Y | 251 | - | 251 | #DIV/0! |
| Z | 4,316 | 9,007 | (4,692) | -52.09% |

Since $c=(C/X)$ then $C=Xc$ and since $q=(C-P)/X$, then $(C-P)=Xq$ or $C=Xq+P$. It means that $(C=C)$ or $Xc=Xq+P$, so $(Xc-Xq)=P$ or $X(c-q)=P$, then $X=P/(c-q)=4,316/(120\%-100\%)=(4,316/20\%)=21,578$.

So, $C=Xc=21,578\times120\%=25,893$ and the quoted long-term debt $(Q)=(L-X)=27,218-21,578=5,641$. If it needs good or trade account payable days $(g)=180$, its good payable $(G)=(Vg/360)=34,524\times180/360=17,262$.

### Accounting *Osaka*[234] of Mitsui Architecture

So then its zero trade related xpress debt that must be paid quickly (**Z**)= (**X-G**)=21,578-17,262=4,316.

| | | | | | | |
|---|---|---|---|---|---|---|
| 43,840 | 36,328 | | | | | |
| latest | 7,512 | 5,667 | | | | |
| | | 1,845 | 496 | | | |
| | | | 1,349 | 955 | | |
| | | | | 394 | (1,208) | - |
| previous | | | | | | - |
| 55,733 | | | | | 1,602 | |

**Mitsui-09**

| | | | | | |
|---|---|---|---|---|---|
| 17,448 | 42,745 | 89,565 | 65,698 | 25,479 | 16,472 |
| 19,894 | | | | | 9,007 |
| 5,403 | | | | 40,219 | |
| | 46,820 | | | 23,867 | 22,265 |
| | | | | 1,602 | |

If it also needs job trade account receivable days (**j**)=120, its job trade account receivables (**J**)=(**Sj/360**)= 46,032x120/360=15,344. So then its kind of cash (**K**)= (**C-J-P**)=25,893-15,344-4,316=6,234. *It's a conservative one.*

So then its total non current, fix and intangible assets (**N**)= (**W-C**)=54,436-25,893=28,643.

Mission accomplished, the finance algebra has identified all **A** to **Z** financial architecture items, coherence with *IFRS* standards, and finance architecture made easy. Is it easier? Hopefullu those help you understand it better.

## Mitsui *Kyoto*[235] Finance Architecture

We shall analyze this suggested Mitsui finance architecture blue-print! Not necessary, but we prove them!

| | | | | |
|---|---|---|---|---|
| 55,733 | 45,616 | | | |
| latest | 10,117 | 6,912 | | |
| | 3,205 | 753 | | |
| | | 2,452 | 1,561 | |
| | | 891 | (907) | - |
| previous | | | | - |
| - | | | 1,798 | |

**Mitsui-08**

| | | | | | |
|---|---|---|---|---|---|
| 18,301 | 43,451 | 84,684 | 65,633 | 28,273 | 15,501 |
| 19,151 | | | | | 12,772 |
| 5,999 | | | | 37,360 | |
| | 41,233 | | 19,051 | 17,253 | |
| | | | | 1,798 | |

The-26 **IFRS'** (*International Finance Reporting Standard*'s) ratios consist of 13 financial architecture <u>key-piles</u>[33] and 13 others <u>locked-stones</u>[34]. The-13 <u>key-piles</u> are:

01: **c**= Current ratio= **(C/X)**=25,893/21,578=**120.00%**

02: **d**= Dividend paid portion to after tax= **(D/A)**=
    838/4,189= **20.00%**, *it's sharp!!*

03: **f**= Fix expenses portion to revenue= **(F/S)**=
    4,603/46,032= **10.00%**, *it's sharp!!*

04: **g**= Goods or trade account payable days= (360**G/V**)=
    360x17,262/34,524=**180.00**, *it's sharp!!*

05: **i**= Investment or financial portion to revenue= (**I/S**)=
   921/46,032=**2.00%**, *it's sharp!!*
06: **j**= Job or trade account receivable days= (360**J/S**)=
   360x15,344/46,032=**120.00**, *it's sharp!!*

|   | 2009 | 2008 | (+) | (%) |
|---|------|------|-----|-----|
| A | 394 | 891 | (497) | -55.78% |
| B | 1,349 | 2,452 | (1,103) | -44.98% |
| C | 42,745 | 43,451 | (706) | -1.62% |
| D | (1,208) | (907) | (301) | 33.19% |
| E | 23,867 | 19,051 | 4,816 | 25.28% |
| F | 5,667 | 6,912 | (1,245) | -18.01% |
| G | 16,472 | 15,501 | 971 | 6.26% |
| H | - | - | - | #DIV/0! |
| I | 496 | 753 | (257) | -34.13% |
| J | 19,894 | 19,151 | 743 | 3.88% |
| K | 17,448 | 18,301 | (853) | -4.66% |
| L | 65,698 | 65,633 | 65 | 0.10% |
| M | 7,512 | 10,117 | (2,605) | -25.75% |

07: **l**= Leverage or gearing = debt equity ratio= *DER*=
   (**L/E**)=27,218/27,218=**100.00%**, *it's sharp!!*
08: **p**= Procurred inventory days= (360**P/V**)=360x4,316
   /34,524=**45.00**, *it's sharp!!*
09: **q**= Quick or acid test ratio= (**C-P**)/**X**=(25,893-4,316)
   /21,578=**100.00%**, *it's sharp!!*

# Mitsui Finance *Yokohama*[237] Architecture

10: **s**= Sales or revenue growth to previous= (S/S'-1)= 46,032/43,840-1=**5.00%**, *it's sharp!!*

|   | 2009 | 2008 | (+) | (%) |
|---|------|------|-----|-----|
| N | 46,820 | 41,233 | 5,587 | 13.55% |
| O | 1,845 | 3,205 | (1,360) | -42.43% |
| P | 5,403 | 5,999 | (596) | -9.93% |
| Q | 40,219 | 37,360 | 2,859 | 7.65% |
| R | 1,602 | 1,798 | (196) | -10.90% |
| S | 43,840 | 55,733 | (11,893) | -21.34% |
| T | 955 | 1,561 | (606) | -38.82% |
| U | 22,265 | 17,253 | 5,012 | 29.05% |
| V | 36,328 | 45,616 | (9,288) | -20.36% |
| W | 89,565 | 84,684 | 4,881 | 5.76% |
| X | 25,479 | 28,273 | (2,794) | -9.88% |
| Y | - | - | - | #DIV/0! |
| Z | 9,007 | 12,772 | (3,765) | -29.48% |

11: **t**= Tax rate or portion to before tax earnings= (T/B)= 1,795/5,984=**30.00%**, *it's sharp!!*
12: **v**= Variable expenses portion to revenue= (V/S)= 34,524/46,032=**75.00%**, *it's sharp!!*
13: **y**= Yielding tax of the dividend paid= (Y/D)=251 /838= **30.00%**, *it's sharp!!*

All 13 (thirteen) *key-pile* finance architecture ratios can be set sharp, and guaranted to perform accurately sharp

# <u>Accounting *Nagasaki*[238] of Mitsui Architecture</u>

The 13 (thirteen) *locked-stone* finance architecture ratios just a derivative of its *key-piles* ratio and not sharp.

|   | 2009 | 2008 | (+) | (%) |
|---|---|---|---|---|
| c | 167.77% | 153.68% | 14.08% | 9.16% |
| d | -306.60% | -101.80% | -204.80% | 201.19% |
| f | 12.93% | 12.40% | 0.52% | 4.23% |
| g | 163.23 | 122.33 | 40.90 | 33.43% |
| i | 1.13% | 1.35% | -0.22% | -16.26% |
| j | 163.36 | 123.70 | 39.66 | 32.06% |
| l | 275.27% | 344.51% | -69.24% | -20.10% |
| p | 53.54 | 47.34 | 6.20 | 13.09% |
| q | 146.56% | 132.47% | 14.09% | 10.64% |
| s | -21.34% | | | |
| t | 70.79% | 63.66% | 7.13% | 11.20% |
| v | 82.86% | 81.85% | 1.02% | 1.24% |
| y | 0.00% | 0.00% | 0.00% | #DIV/0! |

01: **a**= After tax return on asset= (**A/W**)=4,189/54,436 =**7.70%**

02: **b**= Before tax return on asset= (**B/W**)=5,984/44,436 =**10.99%**

03: **e**= Equity return= return on equity= *ROE*= (**R/E**)= 3,351/27,218=**12.31%**

04: **h**= Home taken dividend to utilized equity= (**H/U**)= 585/23,867=**2.46%**

# Mitsui *Sapporo*[239] Finance Architecture

05. **k**= Kind of cash liquidity ratio= **(K/X)**=6,234/21,578
    =**28.89%**

|   | 2009 | 2008 | (+) | (%) |
|---|------|------|-----|-----|
| a | 0.44% | 1.05% | -0.61% | -58.19% |
| b | 1.51% | 2.90% | -1.39% | -47.98% |
| e | 6.71% | 9.44% | -2.73% | -28.88% |
| h | 0.00% | 0.00% | 0.00% | #DIV/0! |
| k | 68.48% | 64.73% | 3.75% | 5.79% |
| m | 48.95% | 65.81% | -16.87% | -25.63% |
| n | 3.65% | 3.23% | 0.43% | 13.27% |
| o | 2.06% | 3.78% | -1.72% | -45.57% |
| r | 1.79% | 2.12% | -0.33% | -15.76% |
| u | 7.20% | 10.42% | -3.23% | -30.96% |
| w | (53.67) | (48.71) | (4.96) | 10.18% |
| x | 38.78% | 43.08% | -4.30% | -9.97% |
| z | 13.71% | 19.46% | -5.75% | -29.55% |

06. **m**= Market-run or asset turn-over= *ATO*= **(S/W)**=
    46,032/54,436=**84.56%**
07. **n**= NPM= net profit margin= **(R/S)**=3,351/46,032
    =**7.28%**
08. **o**= Operational surplus to asset return= **(O/W)**=6,905
    /54,436=**12.68%**
09. **r**= Return of net earnings on assets= *ROA*= **(R/W)**=
    3,351/54,436=**6.16%**

## *Kobe*[240] **Mitsui Accounting Architecture**

The remaining 4 (four) locked-stone finance architecture ratios are as follow:

10: **u**= Utilized return on starting equity= **(R/U)**= 3,351 /23,867=**14.04%**

11: **w**= Working capital days required= **(g-p-j)**=180.00-45.00-120.00=**15.00**, *supplier financed!*

12: **x**= Xpress or current to total debt portion= **(X/L)**= 21,578/27,218=**79.28%**

13: **z**= Zero trade liability portion of total debts= **(Z/L)**= 4,316/27,218= **15.86%**

*What are similarities and differences between the finance architecture and geometric finance?* They both working with visuals and both give significant additional comprehension to the classical finace in nice, easy, short and simple creative method to explain Paccioli's law.. Architecture mostly use geometric skills, but add them with arts, aesthetical composition and specific human interests.

*Can we see the geometric finance a glance to give us better base for analyssis?* Amazon.com is selling our Magic of Geometric Finance book, but we will provide you its summary of useful principles in the next chapter.

*How about the Japanese and global culture involving the architecture? Can we learn some?* Amazon.com is selling our Arigato, Obrigado…(Thanks) historic novel, about Portuguese in Japan in 1550-1647.

*What is the most difficult part in composing finance architecture?* **(A to Z)** and **(a to z)**, they must be unique, short, algebraic, meaningful and not confusing each other.

*Could finance architecture be adopted, used, respected and beneficial?* Sure, after people changed from difficult complex conventional finance to a sharper one!

## CHAPTER-XVI: FINANCE GEOMETRY RESUME

**Money**, (whether people like it or it) had been the most important thing in earth today. Sure, money is not everything, but without it, everything will be very difficult. There are 1001 reasons that a lady want to mary a man, and the first one is money. Off course there are 1000 other reasons which are not money, but the total determinantions of all the 1000 other reason is less than 49%. Money as the first reason is still more than 51% determinations to all the possibilities. *Wonderful*!!

Because of that, the **finance** or money matters, is the most dominant factor of our world economic today. The most important subject in economy suppose to be real **accounting**, not macro concepts and nor managerial tricks and method.

Regretfully this fact is denied by the most prestigious authority. The *Sveriges Riksbank* Prize in Economic Sciences in Memory of Alfred Nobel has been awarded 41 times to 64 Laureates between 1969 and 2009.[1] Most of them are macro economists or even just mathematicians who developed mostly complex but **irrelevant** serial statistical analysis of regressions and corellations which just guessing but could not significantly solving our important real economic and financial problems.

To make our world better, we must first solve the real **finance** and **economic** problems, which are now buried below heavy unuseful difficult complex formats commonly used world-wide. Those can only make genius, average and stupid people lost in the irrelevant complexities.

It's a good news that the **geniuses** and **stupid** people now can understand it better, while the **average** persons are still hard to accept the reality.

The first and most important matter in what ever complex financial matter is **CARE**. Yes, definitely you must handle it with **CARE**. Aside from its fundamental meaning, the word **CARE** here, is a very important abbreviation in finance (**C**= *Capital*, **A**= *Assets*, **R**= *Revenue* and **E**= *Earnings*).

Even the cleverest most finance professor could not make any useful financial analysis, if they do not know the **CARE**. After understanding the **CARE**, you better throw out all of your financial analysis books, because you are now having a more easy and nice but very powerful **synthetical** and **analytical** analysis in strategic corporate finance **geometry**.

After you know your **CARE** very well, you can have a complete financial geometric platform of **CADREX** by computing the **D**= Debt= (**C-A**) and the **X**= Xpenses= (**R-E**). Now you know the complete geometric financial statements of strategic Balance-sheet ("*B/S*")= **CAD** and strategic Income Statement ("*I/S*")= **REX**, architecturally shown as follows:

Balance Sheet (also written as "*B/S*")= **CAD**

| A | **D=(A-C)** |
|---|---|
| "assets" | C |

Income Statement (also written as "*I/S*")= **REX**

| R | **X=(R-E)** |
|---|---|
| "revenue" | E |

After completing the strategic geometric financial statement of **CADREX**, now you can be ready to measure the corporate's *Profitability*, *Liquidity* and *Stability* accurately.

The **CADREX** strategic financial geometric statements is the latest concepts in finance that complied with both the new *IFRS= International Finance Reporing Standards*, and the old *GAAP= Generally Accepted Accounting Principles* that used by financial practitioners and professors world-wide.

The Corporate's <u>Profitability</u>, commonly measured by 3 (three) most important financial ratios as follows:

(1) **n**= **NPM**= *Net Profit Margin*= (**E**/**R**), measuring the Profit (**E**= Earnings) portion, relatively compared to its Total Income (**R**= Revenue), the <u>greater</u> **NPM**, means the corporate's revenue produce <u>better profitability</u> or <u>better income efficiency</u>.

(2) **ROA**= *Return on Assets*= (**E**/**A**), measuring the Profit (**E**= Earnings) portion, relatively compared to its Total Worth (**A**= Assets), the <u>greater</u> **ROA**, means the corporate's assets produce <u>better profitability</u> or <u>better assets efficiency</u>.

(3) **e**= **ROE**= *Return on Equity*= (**E**/**C**), measuring the Profit (**E**= Earnings) portion, relatively compared to its Equity (**C**= Capital), the <u>greater</u> the **ROE**, means the corporate gives <u>better profitability</u> to its <u>owners</u>.

The Corporate's <u>Liquidity</u>, commonly measured by 3 (three) most important financial ratios as follows:

(1) **o**= **ATO**= *Asset Turn-over*= (**R**/**A**), measuring the Total Income (**R**= Revenue) portion, relatively compared to its Total Worth (**A**= Assets), the <u>greater</u> the **ATO**, means the corporate gives <u>better liquidity</u> and <u>faster business movements</u>.

(2) **DER**= *Debt Equity Ratio*= (**D**/**C**), measuring the Liabilities (**D**= Debt) portion, relatively compared to its Equity (**C**= Capital), <u>smaller</u> **DER**, means the corporate's capital gives <u>better liquidity</u> or <u>better payment capability</u>. Best **DER** is slightly greater, but close to 1.00 about 1.01 (Debt <= Capital).

(3) **DAR**= *Debt Asset Ratio*= (**D**/**A**), measuring the Liabilities (**D**= Debt) portion, compared to its Total Worth (**A**= Assets), the <u>smaller</u> **DAR**, means the corporate's capital gives <u>better payment capability</u>. Best **DAR** is about 49,99%.

The Corporate's <u>Stability</u>, commonly measured by 2 (two) most important financial ratios as **CAR** and **X/R**:

(1) **CAR**= *Capital Asset Ratio*= (**C**/**A**), measuring the Equity (**C**= Capital) portion, relatively compared to its Total Worth (**A**= Assets), the <u>greater</u> the **CAR**, means the corporate gives <u>better stability</u> and <u>less dependency to its creditors</u>.

(2) **X/R**= *Xpense to Revenue Ratio*= (**X/R**), measuring the Total Cost (**X**= Xpenses) portion, relatively compared to its Total Income (**R**= Revenue), the <u>smaller</u> **X/R**, means the corporate's capital gives <u>better stability</u> or <u>better efficiency</u>.

When it comes to group consolidation (supposing all the currency and financial dates are equal), the **CARE** must be totalized, then the **D** and **X** computed to becoming the group **CADREX**. Then the others can be completed: (1) **NPM**= (**E/R**), (2) **ROA**= (**E/A**), (3) **ROE**= (**E/C**), (4) **ATO**= (**R/A**), (5) **DER**= (**D/C**), (6) **DAR**= (**D/A**), (7) **CAR**= (**C/A**), and (8) **X/R**= (**X/R**).

If the corporate or group (entity) had set already have the **C**, now targeting the **one** (**ATO**, **NPM** and **ROE**) first, then we may compute: (1) **E**= **Ce**, (2) **R**= **E/n** and (3) **A**= **R/o** then (4) **X**= **R-E**, (5) **D**= **A-C**, (6) **ROA**= (**E/A**), (7) **DER**= (**D/C**), (8) **DAR**= (**D/A**), (9) **CAR**= (**C/A**), and (10) **X/R**= (**X/R**). Those nice and easy process had make you capable to determine the financial performance before (not after) the fact. *Congratulation, not so many people can do financial synthesis!*

# CHAPTER-XVII: EXAMINING SKILLS GAINED

Have you really check the <u>original financial statements</u> and publicized in their information web? Did you <u>really print</u> them after carefully looking at them?

We strongly <u>suggest you to print all</u> of them and <u>attach</u> those to be the compliment of this nice, thin and simple book. So the you can show the world that this book is just simple and thin, but explaining many things much clearer than all the difficult format and analysis commonly used in finance today.

This treatise is <u>significantly different</u> with any other finance book in this world. It even <u>contrasting</u>, but it tells the same world's problematic situation. Much <u>shorter, clearer</u> and more meaningful, <u>better solution</u> for same finance problem.

<u>Finance geometry</u> makes the problem understood better before suggesting solutions for solving them. It's just a luck that we pushed all the finance <u>prejudices and stereotypes out</u>, to make the situation clearer to its readers.

People could not <u>understand</u> it <u>better</u> and <u>faster</u> if using the same approach again and again. Our Napier's box approach has made the situations clearer, and easir to be solved better.

It is just like a wall dividing three filelds, one on the West (let's say **R** field) and two on its East (let's say them **E** and **X** fields).. The length of the wal is always the same, while measured from the West or East. It means that the total length of the two field in the East is equal to the length of one field in the West. If two among those three lengths are known, the we could also know the other missing one. Since **R**=(**X**+**E**), then **E**=(**R**-**X**) and **X**=(**R**-**E**) respectively. *Please compare to theirs!*

# Summary: *Licensing* the Finance *Architects*

Architecture is tough matter, 90% of them will easily pass professional finance exams after learning 2 (two) year in finance. They can even pass with flying colors, in 1 (one) month, if seriously refer to this book and the geometric finance one, especially if they keep themselves independent from unuseful finace myths.

Financial experts are smart people in arithmethics (x,:,+,-), more developed on the numerical rather than spatial intelligence, so then must seriously learn the visual tools for making their finance analysis sharper and faster.

Finance architects are only few people who can understand both and able to explain the financial essence in a nice, short and simple way, covering the essence quickly to the public (*vox populi vox dei*).

Like the building safety, finance architecture must pass all the standard of corporate healthiness and never let any one hide in bulki complex arithmetics. Its summary must be easy, because sum of a million number will be just a number, not a thousand of number.

So please, get the approval from the architectural authotity (like the AIA= American Institute of Architects, RIBA= Royal Institute of British Architects, etc.), before claiming irrelevant non-visuals as architecture. *Always!*

# References (End Notes Bibliographies)

[1] On June 8-9 Clay Mathematics Institute held a conference in Paris to celebrate the resolution of the Poincaré conjecture by Grigoriy Perelman. http://www.claymath.org/;

[2] Grigori Yakovlevich Perelman (Russian: Григо́рий Я́ковлевич Перельма́н, English pronunciation: / pɛrilma n/ *PERR-il-mahn*; born on 13 June 1966), sometimes known as Grisha Perelman, is a Jewish Russian mathematician, who has made landmark contributions to Riemannian geometry and geometric topology. In particular, he proved Thurston's geometrization conjecture. This solves in the affirmative the Poincaré conjecture, posed in 1904, which before its solution was viewed as one of the most important and difficult open problems in topology. http://en.wikipedia.org/wiki/Grigori_Perelman;

[3] Consider a compact 3-dimensional manifold V without boundary. Is it possible that the fundamental group of V could be trivial, even though V is not homeomorphic to the 3-dimensional sphere? Every simply connected, closed 3-manifold is homeomorphic to the 3-sphere. http://en.wikipedia.org/wiki/Poincar%C3%A9_conjecture;

[4] Technique used to determine how different values of an independent variable will impact a particular dependent variable under a given set of assumptions. This technique is used within specific boundaries that will depend on one or more input variables, such as the effect that changes in interest rates will have on a bond's price. Sensitivity analysis is a way to predict the outcome of a decision if a situation turns out to be different compared to the key prediction(s). Investopedia explains *Sensitivity Analysis.*

Sensitivity analysis is very useful when attempting to determine the impact the actual outcome of a particular variable will have if it differs from what was previously assumed. By creating a given set of scenarios, the analyst can determine how changes in one variable(s) will impact the target variable.

For example, an analyst might create a financial model that will value a company's equity (the dependent variable) given the amount of earnings per share (an independent variable) the company reports at the end of the year and the company's price-to-earnings multiple (another independent variable) at that time.

The analyst can create a table of predicted price-to-earnings multiples and a corresponding value of the company's equity based on different values for each of the independent variables. http://www.investopedia.com/terms/s/sensitivityanalysis.asp;

*Steve Asikin: Wonder of Finance ARCHITECTURE*     193

[5] Capital Budgeting Analysis (xls) - Basic program for doing capital budgeting analysis with inclusion of opportunity costs, working capital requirements, etc. http://www.exinfm.com/free_spreadsheets.html;

[6] Aswath *Damodaran,* is a Professor of Finance at the Stern School of Business at New York University, where he teaches corporate finance and equity valuation. http://pages.stern.nyu.edu/~adamodar/; http://www.en.wikipedia.org/wiki/Aswath_Damodaran;

[7] Expert applaud the use of differential *geometry* to integrate the disparate approaches to hedging and risk management. This approach is quite literally. http://www.*www.amazon.com* ›*Books* ›*Business & Investing* › *Finance;*

[8] The aim of the paper is to provide insights into the required *finance architecture* for technology development and transfer on post-2012 agreement. http://iopscience.iop.org/1755-1315/6/27/272005/pdf/ees9_6_272005.pdf; We live and work in turbulent times. Today's global financial world does not resemble anything like that of the late 1940s and 1950s, yet in many respects we have the same regulatory architecture in place. The mismatch between the new reality and the old framework has meant that financial crises have had devastating effects: companies go bankrupt, wealth is destroyed, entire financial systems collapse, and economic growth is impaired for years. http://www.mckinsey.com/ideas/mitt/anfa/;

[9] The *American Institute of Architects* (*AIA*) is a professional organization for architects in the United States. Headquartered in Washington, D.C. http://www.aia.org; http://www.en.wikipedia.org/wiki/American_Institute_of_Architects;

[10] Many of the standards forming part of IFRS are known by the older name of International Accounting Standards (IAS). IAS were issued between 1973 and 2001 by the Board of the International Accounting Standards Committee (IASC). On 1 April 2001, the new IASB took over from the IASC the responsibility for setting International Accounting Standards.
  During its first meeting the new Board adopted existing IAS and SICs. The IASB has continued to develop standards calling the new standards IFRS. http://en.wikipedia.org/wiki/International_Financial_Reporting_Standards;

[11] Enron filed for bankruptcy protection in the Southern District of New York in late 2001 and selected Weil, Gotshal & Manges as its bankruptcy counsel. It emerged from bankruptcy in November 2004, pursuant to a court-approved

plan of reorganization, after one of the biggest and most complex bankruptcy cases in U.S. history. http://en.wikipedia.org/wiki/Enron;

[12] In July 2006, the European Commission established a Standards Advice Review Group (SARG) in the area of accounting "to ensure objectivity and proper balance of the European Financial Reporting Advisory Group's (EFRAG) opinions". The Group will be composed of independent experts and high-level representatives from National Standard Setters whose experience and competence in accounting are widely recognised. The Group's task will be to assess whether the endorsement advice given by the EFRAG is well balanced and objective. http://www.iasplus.com/restruct/resteuro.htm#process;

[13] U.K, U.S.A and China. Analysis of these different accounting systems will be conducted on issues such as growth and background, social, economic and fiscal pressures that have led to each nations current characteristics. Concluding on the direction each nations accounting systems and practices seem to be heading towards. Introduction The main characteristics of U.K accounting is that it is highly dominated by organised accounting profession, which only relate to limited liability companies, no other such entity. A separate fiscal accounting has been developed entirely from commercial accounting. Public sector in the U.K follows its own different rules in accounting. http://www.echeat.com/essay.php?t=26973;

[14] The adage "A *picture* is worth a *thousand words*" refers to the idea that a complex idea can be conveyed with just a single still image. It also aptly characterizes one of the main goals of visualization, namely making it possible to absorb large amounts of data quickly. It is believed that the modern use of the phrase stems from an article by Fred R. Barnard in the advertising trade journal *Printers' Ink*, promoting the use of images in advertisements that appeared on the sides of streetcars. The December 8, 1921 issue carries an ad entitled, "One Look is Worth A Thousand Words." Soon after, the proverb would become popularly attributed to *Confucius*.

http://www.en.wikipedia.org/wiki/A_picture_is_worth_a_thousand_words;

[15] The Sveriges Riksbank Prize in *Economic* Sciences in Memory of Alfred *Nobel* has been awarded 41 times to 64 *Laureates* between 1969 and 2009. http://www.nobelprize.org/nobel_prizes/economics/laureates/;

[16] Today's accounting and finance professional faces a number of challenges. Business transactions are becoming increasingly complex, as are the accounting standards that may apply. Accounting for transactions

incorrectly can have significant consequences, and the current regulatory environment discourages asking the external auditor for help to figure out the accounting. You need an objective resource that understands complex transactions and the authoritative literature that may apply.
http://www.huronconsultinggroup.com/service.aspx?serviceId=921;

[17] All About Skyscrapers.com is a online database of skyscraper articles geared toward educating the public about all aspects of the skyscraper. As the skyscraper becomes increasingly important, it is vital the public understands the fundamentals of the development, financing and operation of skyscrapers. We hope you enjoy the information we have collected and find it useful.
http://www.allaboutskyscrapers.com/;

[18] Samsung (Korea) 2009:
http://www.samsung.com/us/aboutsamsung/ir/financialinformation/auditedfinancialstatements/downloads/parent/2009_end04_eng_bs.pdf;
http://www.samsung.com/us/aboutsamsung/ir/financialinformation/auditedfinancialstatements/downloads/parent/2009_end04_eng_soi.pdf;

[19] Physical or "tangible cultural heritage" includes buildings and historic places, monuments, artifacts, etc., that are considered worthy of preservation for the future. These include objects significant to the archaeology, architecture, science or technology of a specific culture. Heritage can also include cultural landscapes (natural features that may have cultural attributes) Recently heritage practitioners have moved from classifying heritage as natural as man has intervened in the shaping of nature in the past four million years.

http://en.wikipedia.org/wiki/Cultural_heritage;

[20] The technique of measuring quantities from drawings, sketches and specifications prepared by designers, principally architects and engineers, in order to prepare tender/contract documents, is known in the industry as taking off. The quantities of work taken off typically are used to prepare bills of quantities, which usually are prepared in accordance with a published standard method of measurement (SMM) as agreed to by the QS profession and representatives of the construction industry. Many larger QS firms have their own in-house methods of measurement and most bills of quantities prepared today are in an abbreviated format from the one required by the SMM.
http://en.wikipedia.org/wiki/Quantity_surveyor;

[21] Megastructures are an architectural concept popularized in the 1960s where a city could be encased in a single building, or a relatively small number of buildings interconnected together. The concept was popularized by avant-garde architectural groups such as Archigram. http://en.wikipedia.org/wiki/Megastructures_%28architecture%29;

[22] In the fields of *architecture* and civil engineering, construction is a process that consists of many items, the design usually consists of drawings and *specifications*, as the legal basis of drawings and a bill of *quantities* provided by a *quantity* surveyor. http://www.en.wikipedia.org/wiki/Construction;

[23] A *blueprint* is a type of paper-based reproduction usually of a technical drawing, documenting an architecture or an *engineering* design. http://www.en.wikipedia.or g/wiki/Blueprint;

[24] *CAD*: *Architectural* Engineering Construction (AEC) ... An architectural parametric 3D CAD that allows you to create three-dimensional elements. http://www.caddprimer.com/cad .../cad_lab_architectural_software.htm

[25] Boeing (USA) 2009:
http://www.boeing.com/news/releases/2010/q1/100127a_nr.pdf;

[26] Wall-Mart (USA) 2009:
http://walmartstores.com/sites/AnnualReport/2009/financials.html;
http://moneycentral.msn.com/investor/invsub/results/statemnt.aspx?symbol=wmt
http://www.annualreports.com/HostedData/AnnualReports/PDFArchive/wmt2009.pdf;

[27] Mac Donald (USA) 2009:
http://moneycentral.msn.com/investor/invsub/results/statemnt.aspx?symbol=MCD;

[28] Microsoft (USA) 2009: http://finance.yahoo.com/q/is?s=msft&annual;
http://finance.yahoo.com/q/bs?s=MSFT+Balance+Sheet&annual;
http://www.microsoft.com/investor/reports/ar09/10k_fr_not_21.html;
http://www.annualreports.com/HostedData/AnnualReports/PDFArchive/10k_fr
_inc.html http://www.microsoft.com/investor/reports/ar09/10k_fh_fin.html;
http://moneycentral.msn.com/investor/invsub/results/statemnt.aspx?symbol=msft

[29] Misubishi (Japan) 2009:
http://www.mitsubishi-motors.com/corporate/ir/financial/e/;
http://www.mitsubishi-motors.com/corporate/ir/share/pdf/e/kessan/100607.pdf;
http://www.mitsubishi-motors.com/corporate/ir/share/pdf/e/annual0410.pdf;
http://www.mitsubishi-motors.com/corporate/ir/share/pdf/e/kessan/100607.pdf;
http://www.hotstocked.com/companies/m/mitsubishi-ufj-financial-group-inc-MBFJF-balance-sheet-93109.html;

[30] Sumitomo-Mitsui (Japan) 2009:
http://finance.yahoo.com/q/is?s=MITSY+Income+Statement&annual;
http://finance.yahoo.com/q/bs?s=MITSY+Balance+Sheet&annual;
http://www.smfg.co.jp/english/investor/financial/latest_statement/pdf/e_09073
0.pdf; http://finance.yahoo.com/q/bs?s=MITSY&annual;

[31] Hyundai (Korea) 2009:
http://worldwide.hyundai.com/company-overview/in;
http://worldwide.hyundai.com/company-overview/investor-relations/financial-information-statements-balance-sheets.aspx;
http://worldwide.hyundai.com/company-overview/investor-relations/financial-information-statements-income-view.aspx?idx=110&strPartValue=IS&nCurPage=1&strSearchColumn=&strSearchWord=&ListNum=26;

[32] Daimler Benz (Germany) 2009:
http://www.daimler.com/Projects/c2c/channel/documents/1812642_DAI_2009
_Annual_Financial_Statements_Daimler_AG__Einzelabschluss_.pdf;
http://www.daimler.com/Projects/c2c/channel/documents/1813321_DAI_2009
_Annual_Report.pdf; http://ar2009.daimler.com/en/consolidated-financial-statements/statement-of-income.html;

[33] BMW (Germany) 2009:
http://www.bmwgroup.com/e/0_0_www_bmwgroup_com/investor_relations/co
rporate_events/hauptversammlung/2010/_pdf/BMW_AG_Jahresabschluss_engl
.pdf;

[34] British Petroleum (UK) 2009:
http://www.bp.com/liveassets/bp_internet/globalbp/STAGING/global_assets/d
ownloads/B/bp_fourth_quarter_and_full_year_2009_results.pdf;
http://www.bp.com/assets/bp_internet/globalbp/globalbp_uk_english/set_branc
h/STAGING/common_assets/downloads/pdf/BP_Annual_Report_and_Account
s_2009_Financial_Statements.pdf;

[35] Carefour (French):
http://www.carrefour.com/docroot/groupe/C4com/Pieces_jointes/RA/COMMU
NIQUE%20FINAL%20RA09UK.pdf;

[36] Nestle (Swiss) 2009:
http://www.nestle.com/InvestorRelations/Investor+Relations.htm
http://search.yahoo.com/search;_ylt=A0oGdDLU6mNMOycBiu5XNyoA;_ylc
=X1MDMjc2NjY3OQRfcgMyBGZyA3VzaDEtZmluYW5jZQRmcjIIDc2EtZ3
AEZ3ByaWQDBGhvc3RwdmlkA3lsMEYuMG9HZEl3dkRsaTNTemxhV1FZ
eVRVTi5iMHhqNnRRQUNvLloEbl9ncHMDMTAEbl92cHMDMARvcmlna
W4Dc3JwBHBvcwMxBHBxc3RyAzIwMDkgZmluYW5jaWFsIHN0YXRlbW
VudARxdWVyeQMyMDA5IGZpbmFuY2lhbCBzdGF0ZW1lbnQgb2YgbmVz
dGxlBHNhYwMxBHNhbwMxBHZ0ZXN0aWQDRjY1NA--
?p=2009%20financial%20statement%20of%20nestle&fr=ush1-
finance&fr2=sg-gac&sado=1&pqstr=2009%20financial%20statement;
http://search.yahoo.com/search;_ylt=A0oGdEEM7mNMhhoBOV1XNyoA;_yl
c=X1MDMjc2NjY3OQRfcgMyBGFvAzEEZnIDdXNoMS1maW5hbmNlBGh
vc3RwdmlkA0ZzRnRjRW9HZEl3dkRsaTNTemxhV1JBUmdQRmJEMHhqN
2d3QUFSUWcEbl9ncHMDMARuX3ZwcwMwBG9yaWdpbgNzcnAEcXVlcn
kDbmVzdGxlIDIwMDkgZmluYW5jaWFsIHN0YXRlbWVudARzYW8DMQ
R2dGVzdGlkA0Y2NTQ-?p=nestle+2009+financial+statement&fr2=sb-
top&fr=ush1-financevestor-relations/financial-information-statements-balance-
sheets-
view.aspx?idx=111&strPartValue=BS&nCurPage=1&strSearchColumn=&strS
earchWord=&ListNum=26;;

[37] *Pile.* A deep foundation. These are formed by creating a hole deep enough
to locate solid sub-soil. The hole is usually filled with concrete and reinforced.
http://www.*en.mimi.hu; › Architecture;*
Pile foundations are the part of a structure used to carry and transfer the load of
the structure to the bearing ground located at some depth below ground surface.
The main components of the foundation are the pile cap and the piles. Piles are
long and slender members which transfer the load to deeper soil or rock of high
bearing capacity avoiding shallow soil of low bearing capacity The main types
of materials used for piles are Wood, steel and concrete. Piles made from these
materials are driven, drilled or jacked into the ground and connected to pile
caps. Depending upon type of soil, pile material and load transmitting
characteristic piles are classified accordingly. In the following chapter we learn
about, classifications, functions and pros and cons of piles.
http://en.wikipedia.org/wiki/Foundation_%28engineering%29;

[38] Instead, the rooms that the walls housed were made to be *locked* from the
inside. Pyramids have occasionally been used.
http://en.wikipedia.org/wiki/Pyramid;

<sup>39</sup> In mathematics, two vectors are *orthogonal* if they are perpendicular, i.e., they form a right angle. The word comes from the Greek ὀρθός (orthos), http://www.en.wikipedia.org/wiki/Orthogonality

<sup>40</sup> *Geodesy* also named geodetics, a branch of earth sciences, is the scientific discipline that deals with the measurement and representation of the Earth, http://www.en.wikipedia.org/wiki/Geodesy;

<sup>41</sup> Using geology as a model for architecture. In reference to "Collage City"- Colin Rowe, Fred Koetter. I believe that within geology, or the understanding of the collage of the fragments of universal evolution, we can further understand the role of architecture. The attempt here is to begin the crawl out of the pond, with the use of geological markings (organic and inorganic special relationships). http://www.designcommunity.com/discussion/8089.html;

<sup>42</sup> ('söil mi'kan·iks) (*engineering*) The application of the laws of solid and fluid mechanics to soils and similar granular materials as a basis for design, construction, and maintenance of stable foundations and earth structures. http://www.answers.com/topic/soil-mechanics;

<sup>43</sup> *Structural engineering* is a field of engineering dealing with the analysis and design of structures that support or resist loads. http://www.google.co.id/#hl=en&q=structure+engineering&aq=f&aqi=g3g-m1g-ms1g-m2g-ms1&aql=&oq=&gs_rfai=&fp=ce904cf19dd62137;

<sup>44</sup> Pile foundations have been used as load carrying and load transferring systems for many years. In the early days of civilisation[2], from the communication, defence or strategic point of view villages and towns were situated near to rivers and lakes. It was therefore important to strengthen the bearing ground with some form of piling. http://en.wikipedia.org/wiki/Foundation_%28engineering%29;

<sup>45</sup> The intersection of two vaulting surfaces, with consistency of a bituminous material expressed as the distance (in hundredths of a centimeter) that a standard needle vertically penetrates a sample of the material under known conditions of loading, time, and temperature. Unless otherwise specified, the load, time, and temperature are understood to be 100 g, 5 sec, and 25°C (77°F), respectively. http://www.answers.com/topic/penetration;

[46] At a construction site, a temporary framework used in hoisting building components or equipment. http://www.answers.com/topic/erection-tower;

[47] Because *Pacioli* was a Franciscan friar, he might be referred to simply as Friar *Luca*. While Friar *Luca* is often called the "Father of *Accounting*," he did the trial balance (summa summarium) for the end of *Pacioli's accounting* cycle. http://www.en.wikipedia.org/wiki/Luca_Pacioli; http://www.www.riley-smith.com/hamish/document_view.php?cat=1; http://www.historiabooks.blogspot.com/.../summa-de-arithmetica-luca-paccioli.html;

[48] In architecture and building construction, any isolated, vertical structural member such as a pier, column, or post. It may be constructed of a single piece of stone or wood or built up of units, such as bricks. It may be any shape in cross section. A pillar commonly has a load-bearing or stabilizing function, but it may also stand alone, as do commemorative pillars. *See also* column, http://www.britannica.com/EBchecked/topic/460521/pillar; A column in structural engineering is a vertical structural element that transmits, through compression, the weight of the structure above to other structural elements below. For the purpose of wind or earthquake engineering, columns may be designed to resist lateral forces. Other compression members are often termed "columns" because of the similar stress conditions. Columns are frequently used to support beams or arches on which the upper parts of walls or ceilings rest. In architecture "column" refers to such a structural element that also has certain proportional and decorative features. A column might also be a decorative or triumphant feature but need not be supporting any structure e.g. a statue on top. http://en.wikipedia.org/wiki/Column;

[49] John Napier's description of what we usually call "*Napier's Bones*" comes to us through the book Rabdology (a term coined by him) or "Calculation with Rods. Http://www.17centurymaths.com/; ./napier/.../Napiers%20Bones/NapiersBones.html

[50] In engineering, originally a solid piece of timber, as a beam of a house, a plow, a loom, or a balance. In building construction, a beam is a horizontal member spanning an opening and carrying a load that may be a brick or stone wall above the opening, in which case the beam is often called a lintel (*see* post-and-lintel system). The load may be a floor or roof in a building, in which case the beam is called a floor joist or a roof joist. In a bridge deck the lightly loaded longitudinal beams. http://www.britannica.com/EBchecked/topic/57229/beam;

[51] A cantilever, also called a fixed end beam, is a beam supported only at one end. The beam cannot rotate in any direction; thus it creates a solid support. The cantilever is considered the third of the three great structural methods, the other two being post-and-beam construction and arch construction. The cantilever thrusts down which is different from the thrust of an arch which is outward against its supports.

http://science.jrank.org/pages/1171/Cantilever.html#ixzz0xuVkkqkH

[52] *Portal* is a general term describing an opening in the walls of a building, gate or fortification, and especially a grand entrance to an important structure.
http://www.en.wikipedia.org/wiki/Portal_(architecture*);*

[53] In elementary mathematics, physics, and engineering, a Euclidean vector (sometimes called a geometric or spatial vector or – as here – simply a vector) is a geometric object that has both a magnitude (or length) and direction. A Euclidean vector is frequently represented by a line segment with a definite direction, or graphically as an arrow, connecting an initial point *A* with a terminal point *B*. http://en.wikipedia.org/wiki/Euclidean_vector;

[54] A deep foundation is used to transfer a load from a structure through an upper weak layer of soil to a stronger deeper layer of soil. There are different types of deep foundations including helical piles, impact driven piles, drilled shafts, caissons, piers, and earth stabilized columns. The naming conventions for different types of foundations vary between different engineers.
http://en.wikipedia.org/wiki/Foundation_%28engineering%29;
A *basement* is one or more floors of a building that are either completely or partially below the ground floor. Basements are typically used as a utility.
http://en.wikipedia.org/wiki/Basement;

[55] Their involvement may include pre-merger planning, crafting the merger governance and architecture, acting as clean teams prior to regulatory approval, running the integration office, and supporting high-impact value capture or functional integration teams. McKinsey offers support for individual acquisitions, past acquisitions that require further integration, and building capability for executing a series of acquisitions.
http://corporatefinance.mckinsey.com/aboutus/ourapproach/cfscom.htm
The redesign of the global financial architecture, and to focus instead on what the private sector – specifically institutional investors and financial

intermediaries – can do collectively to help minimize the frequency and severity of future crises. http://www.mckinsey.com/ideas/mitt/anfa/

[56] Architects decide what the building *looks* like, keeps the lines of the building elegant, makes the building a beautiful and interesting place to be. They take courses in design and architectural history and design the floorplans and appearance of the building. The architects actually usually decide the materials of the building, as well. Architects must be part artists, part pragmatists, and must be brilliant designers.

Competition is cut-throat, and while the payoff can result in both fame and fortune, the majority of architects really struggle at first after their education and internships are through. From there, the architectural plans go the civil (structural) engineer. Within the framework that the architect provides, the structural engineer must design the infrastructure, the skeleton, of the building. http://talk.collegeconfidential.com/architecture-major/64164-difference-between-civil-engineering-architecture.html;

[57] In Greek mythology, the Titans (Greek: Τιτάν - Ti-tan; plural: Τιτᾶνες - Ti-tânes) were a race of powerful deities, descendants of Gaia and Uranus, that ruled during the legendary

Golden Age. http://en.wikipedia.org/wiki/Titan_%28mythology%29;

[58] An *anachronism*—from the Greek ανά (ana: up, against, back, re-) and χρόνος (chronos: time)—is an error in chronology, especially a chronological misplacing. http://www.en.wikipedia.org/wiki/Anachronism;

[59] In various versions of the tale, a group of blind men (or men in the dark) touch an elephant to learn what it is like. Each one feels a different part, but only one part, such as the side or the tusk. They then compare notes and learn that they are in complete disagreement. The stories differ primarily in how the elephant's body parts are described, how violent the conflict becomes and how (or if) the conflict among the non visual men and their perspectives is resolved. http://en.wikipedia.org/wiki/Blind_men_and_an_elephant;

[60] In structural engineering, the Joist is a lightweight steel truss consisting, in the standard form, of parallel chords and a triangulated web system, proportioned to span between bearing points. The main function of a joist is to provide direct support for roof or floor deck and to transfer the load imposed on the deck to the structural frame i.e. beam and column.

http://en.wikipedia.org/wiki/Open_web_steel_joist; .

[61] *Takabeya*, *Fukuhei*, Vertical and horizontal load stresses in the building frames with constant ratio of stiffness.
http://www.eprints.lib.hokudai.ac.jp/dspace/items-by-type?type=bulletin;

[62] Probably the most famous structure in all of *Egypt*, the *Pyramids* are still on of the worlds best *architectural* achievement, even though they were built thousand years ago. http://www.library.thinkquest.org/10098/egypt.htm;

[63] *Architecture* of *Great Wall* of *China* is introduced with evidence and other detail information. the *Great Wall* of *China*. the *Great Wall*. The Chinese call the wall "Wan-Li" Wall, with each watchtower serving as an example of different *architecture*.
http://www.beijingservice.com/attractions/greatwall/architectureindex.htm;

[64] *mastaba* (măs'təbə), in Egyptian *architecture*, a sepulchral structure built aboveground. The *mastabas* of the early dynastic period (3200-2680 B.C.). *Mastaba* tombs surround the pyramids of the Old Kingdom. Courtiers and families of the monarch were buried in these low rectangular brick. decorated with texts and images. www.civilization.ca/cmc/exhibitions/civil;
www.answers.com/topic/mastaba; www.aldokkan.com/art/mastaba.htm;

[65] In Tellugu Edu are seven and *Pailu* is stream. ... The *architecture* and construction of the Thousand Pillar Temple in Warangal is exactly similar.
http://www.overindia.com/category/andhra-pradesh/medak/;

[66] *Tori's* works exemplify *Japanese* Buddhist *art* during the Asuka period. His style ultimately derives from that of the Chinese Wei kingdom of the late 4th.http://www.en.wikipedia.org/wiki/Tori_Busshi

[67] Hyperbolic Paraboloids (Erik Demaine) The term *hypar* was introduced by the *architect* Heinrich Engel in his 1967 ... *Hypars* in *Architecture*. *Hypars* and joining *hypars* in a few http://www.erikdemaine.org/hypar/

[68] geometry should be close to *architectural* design processes and use devices as section and plan to define the *folded plate* structure.

www.shambles.net/pages/learning/MathsP/PaperFold/;
http://www.infoscience.epfl.ch/record/;

[69] Concrete reinforced by either pretensioning or posttensioning, allowing it to carry a greater load or span a greater distance than ordinary reinforced concrete. In pretensioning, lengths of steel wire or cables are laid in the empty mold and stretched. The concrete is placed and allowed to set, and the cables are released, placing the concrete into compression as the steel shrinks back to its original length. In posttensioning, the steel in the concrete is stretched after the curing process. Prestressing places a concrete member in compression; these compressive stresses counteract the tensile bending stresses of an applied load.                http://www.britannica.com/EBchecked/topic/475539/prestressed-concrete;

[70] A tensile structure is a construction of elements carrying only tension and no compression or bending. The term tensile should not be confused with tensegrity, which is a structural form with both tension and compression elements.Most tensile structures are supported by some form of compression or bending elements, such as masts (as in The $O_2$, formerly the Millennium Dome), compression rings or beams. Tensile membrane structures are most often used as roofs as they can economically and attractively span large distances. http://en.wikipedia.org/wiki/Tensile_structure;

[71] *Zeitgeist* is "the spirit of the times" or "the spirit of the age." *Zeitgeist* is the general cultural, intellectual, ethical, spiritual, and/or political. http://www.en.wikipedia.org/wiki/Zeitgeist;

[72] A comprehensive world view (or worldview) is the fundamental cognitive orientation of an individual or society encompassing natural philosophy, fundamental existential and normative postulates or themes, values, emotions, and ethics. The term is a calque of German *Weltanschauung* [ vɛlt.ʔan ˌʃaʊ.ʊŋ] (◀◗ listen), composed of *Welt*, 'world', and *Anschauung*, 'view' or 'outlook'. It is a concept fundamental to German philosophy and epistemology and refers to a *wide world perception*. Additionally, it refers to the framework of ideas and beliefs through which an individual interprets the world and interacts with it. http://en.wikipedia.org/wiki/World_view;

[73] *Monumental architecture*, at an archaeological site, refers to large man-made structures of stone or earth. http://www.archaeology.about.com/cs/glossary/g/monumental.htm;

[74] *colossal* order (*architecture*), *architectural* order extending beyond one interior story, often extending through www.britannica.com/EBchecked/topic/126609/colossal-order;

[75] *Mandala*: The *Architecture* of Enlightenment. "Floorplans of the universe," that is exactly what *mandalas* are called in this introduction to an Asia Society. http://healing.about.com/od/mandalaorigins/Origins_of_Mandalas_and_Mandala_Drawing.htm;

[76] In physics, energy (from the Greek ἐνέργεια - *energeia*, "activity, operation", from ἐνεργός - *energos*, "active, working"[1]) is a quantity that is often understood as the ability to perform work. This quantity can be assigned to any particle, object, or system of objects as a consequence of its physical state. http://en.wikipedia.org/wiki/Energy;

[77] *Gravitational fields* are a method of expressing gravity in terms that make it easy to apply in specific cases. Learn about how *gravitational fields*, http://www.physics.about.com/od/classicalmechanics/a/gravity_2.htm;

[78] *Decomposition* or rotting is the process by which tissues of a dead organism break down into simpler forms of matter. The process is essential for new growth. http://www.en.wikipedia.org/wiki/Decomposition;
Chemical *decomposition*, analysis or breakdown is the separation of a chemical compound into elements or simpler compounds. http://www.en.wikipedia.org/wiki/Chemical_decomposition;

[79] Functional anatomy of a taxon strongly conditions many intrinsic *bone* properties, including *structural* or *bone* mineral density. In order to measure how this.

http://www.linkinghub.elsevier.com/retrieve/pii/S030544030190826X;

[80] The Phoenix (Ancient Greek: Φοῖνιξ, phoínix, Persian: سوندق, Arabic: العنقاء) is a mythical sacred firebird that can be found in the mythologies of the Persians, Greeks, Romans, Egyptians, Chinese, and (according to Sanchuniathon) Phoenicians.

A phoenix is a mythical bird that is a fire spirit with a colorful plumage and a tail of gold and scarlet (or purple, blue, and green according to some legends). It has a 500 to 1000 year life-cycle, near the end of which it builds itself a nest of twigs that then ignites; both nest and bird burn fiercely and are reduced to ashes, from which a new, young phoenix or phoenix egg arises, reborn anew to live again. The new phoenix is destined to live as long as its old self. In some stories, the new phoenix embalms the ashes of its old self in an egg made of myrrh and deposits it in the Egyptian city of Heliopolis (literally "sun-city" in Greek). It is said that the bird's cry is that of a beautiful song. In very few stories they are able to change into people.

http://en.wikipedia.org/wiki/Phoenix_%28mythology%29;

[81] A *storm* (from Proto-Germanic *sturmaz "noise, tumult") is any disturbed state of an astronomical body's atmosphere, especially affecting its surface, http://www.en.wikipedia.org/wiki/Storm

[82] A *storm* (from Proto-Germanic *sturmaz "noise, tumult") is any disturbed state of an astronomical body's atmosphere, especially affecting its surface, http://www.en.wikipedia.org/wiki/Storm;

[83] *Fluid mechanics* is the study of fluids and the forces on them. (Fluids include liquids, gases, and plasmas.).
http://www.en.wikipedia.org/wiki/Fluid_mechanics;

[84] molecules are to be kept from moving from the *surface* into the bulk liquid,. All phenomena in *mechanics* can be explained in terms of either forces or energies. http://www.web.mit.edu/hml/ncfmf/04STFM.pdf;

[85] *Viscosity* is a measure of the resistance of a *fluid* which is being deformed by either shear stress or tensile stress.
http://www.en.wikipedia.org/wiki/Viscosity

[86] *Archimedes screw*, also known as *Archimedes' screw*, the *Archimedean screw* or the screwpump is a machine historically used for transferring water from lower places. http://www.en.wikipedia.org/wiki/Archimedes'_screw;

[87] A *transverse wave* is a moving wave that consists of oscillations occurring perpendicular to the direction of energy transfer.
http://www.en.wikipedia.org/wiki/Transverse_wave;

[88] *Longitudinal waves* are waves that have the same direction of vibration along their direction of travel, which means that the vibration of the medium.
http://www.en.wikipedia.org/wiki/Longitudinal_wave;

[89] *ISO* 9000 is a family of standards for quality management systems. *ISO* 9000 is maintained by *ISO*, the International Organization for Standardization. http://www.en.wikipedia.org/wiki/ISO_9000;

[90] California Fruit Growers Exchange. It adopted the "Sunkist" name in 1908 for its highest quality oranges, and so was the first to brand fruit.Currently representing about 6000 members, Sunkist is a not-for-profit corporation, with all profits from the exchange returned to the growers. Sunkist is the largest marketing cooperative in the world's fruit and vegetable industry, and is one of the 10 largest marketing cooperatives in America. http://en.wikipedia.org/wiki/Sunkist_Growers,_Incorporated#Sunkist_fruit_crat e_label;

[91] Alsace-Lorraine is one of the Germanic lands that has *preserved* the most its traditional Germanic *architecture*, so it's a very interesting. http://www.skyscrapercity.com/showthread.php?t=1156815

[92] *Architects* use these equations to determine measurements for their blueprints. Roofs in peticular require *trigonometry* to find the peak as well as the angle. http://www.zcons.glogster.com/trigonometry-in-architecture/;

[93] *In the Pythagorean tradition, astronomy is interpreted as magnitudes in motion, geometry as magnitudes at rest, arithmetic as numbers absolute, and music as numbers applied.*
*http://www.philophony.com/sensprop/pythagor.html;*

[94] An interdisciplinary course on mathematics in art and *architecture*. The *Platonic solids* and polyhedra have inspired people throughout the ages. http://www.math.nus.edu.sg/aslaksen/teaching/math-art-arch.shtml

[95] Symmetrical *balance* is used extensively in *architecture* and it feels very stable, Even if we cannot move an object in a scene, its visual *weight* can be determined. https://www.siggraph.org/education/

[96] In order to improve the bulb, *Edison* needed all the persistence he had learned years.


http://www.fi.edu/learn/sci.../edison-lightbulb/edison-lightbulb.php

He assisted in *experiments* on the telephone, phonograph. Thomas *Edison's* first successful *light bulb* model, used in public demonstration at Menlo Park, http://www.en.wikipedia.org/wiki/Thomas_Edison

[97] A suspension bridge, by definition is a bridge where cables (ropes or chains), are strung across the river (or whatever the obstacle happens to be) and the deck is suspended from these cables.
http://www.helium.com/knowledge/259396-suspension-bridges;

[98] *architecture*. From small awnings to vast stadiums, membranes easily inspire new forms. connected to a circular concrete *stress ring*.
http://www.multimedia.3m.com/mws/mediawebserver?mwsId;

[99] In masonry, a curved structure that supports the weight of material over an open space, as in a bridge or doorway.
http://www.www.talktalk.co.uk/reference/encyclopaedia;

[100] A *flying buttress* is a specific form of buttressing most strongly associated with gothic church *architecture*. It serves to transmit the lateral forces
http://www.en.wikipedia.org/wiki/Flying_buttress;

[101] *Aqueducts* at Tarragona, Segovia, Spalato, and elsewhere still testify to the importance which the old Romans attached to a good water supply, http://www.oldandsold.com/articles22/architecture-40-a.shtml;

[102] *Landscape architecture* is the design of outdoor and public spaces to achieve environmental, socio-behavioral, and/or aesthetic outcomes.
http://www.en.wikipedia.org/wiki/Landscape_architecture

[103] *Site planning* in landscape architecture and architecture refers to the organizational stage of the landscape design process. It involves the organization. http://www.en.wikipedia.org/wiki/Site_planning

[104] Thomas Church was a mid-century landscape *architect* significant in the profession. His book "*Gardens* Are For People," and numerous campus master planning. http://www.en.wikipedia.org/wiki/Landscape_architecture

[105] Recipes are important, also in urban design (and *architecture*). ... "As long as *planology* does nothing but concern itself with 'practical' problems, http://www.books.google.co.id/books?isbn=0792326199

[106] *Urban design* is derived from but transcends planning and transportation policy, *architectural* design, development economics, engineering and landscape. http://www.urbandesign.org

[107] Three objectives, namely, that of preserving the *architectural* and *townscape* heritage, making it a proper part of the socio-economic future in all parts. http://www.powerofculture.nl/uk/archive

[108] Taking a Chicago *Architectural* Walking Tour is a fantastic way to experience the city and discover the little details that make Chicago great. http://www.gochicago.about.com/.../chicago_downtown_architecture_tour.htm

[109] In addition to the breathtaking *architecture*, the *mall* has incorporated retail zoning. Centrally located in Dubai *City* this *mall* is know for its design, http://www.dubai-architecture.info/DUB-010.htm

[110] Baroque *architecture* is a term used to describe the era, starting in the early 17th century in Italy, that took the humanist Roman vocabulary of Renaissance http://www.en.wikipedia.org/wiki/Baroque_architecture

[111] *Rococo architecture* was a variation of baroque. It began in the eighteenth century at Versailles. It was lighter, more graceful, and more subdued. http://www.library.thinkquest.org/16545/data/low/rococo.htm

[112] *Chichen Itza's architecture* is seen to have two distinctive styles; traditional Mayan architecture, and more recent Toltec architecture. http://www.world-

mysteries.com/chichen_index.htm *Chichén Itzá,* Mexico     Dedicated to the feathered serpent god Kukulcan, this is the most famous landmark of *Chichén Itzá*. http:// www.sacred-destinations.com/mexico/chichen-itza

[113] A keystone is the architectural piece at the crown of a <u>vault</u> or <u>arch</u> which marks its <u>apex</u>, locking the other pieces into position. This makes a keystone very important structurally. In an arch, the keystone is usually larger than the <u>voussoirs</u> that make up the arch and may serve primarily an aesthetic purpose. Some say that a keystone is not as important structurally as the <u>voussoirs</u>, since the removal of any of the voussoirs would cause the arch to collapse but this is not necessarily true of the keystone.
http://en.wikipedia.org/wiki/Keystone_%28architecture%29

[114] *Dolmens* can be found across Portugal, from simple ones  to the more complex examples of megalithic *architecture*, such as the Almendres Cromlech. http://www.answers.com/topic/dolmen

[115] *Experimental Architecture* is a branch of the architectural discipline concerned with the development of conceptual projects challenging conventional. http://www.en.wikipedia.org/wiki/Experimental_Architecture

[116] Building *Engineering Physics* is unique from other established applied sciences or engineering professions as it combines the sciences of *architecture*.
http://.www.en.wikipedia.org/wiki/Building_Engineering_Physics

[117] Dmitri *Mendeleev* formulated a periodic table similar to the one we use today. Elements were grouped according to recurring trends in their properties. http://www.chemistry.about.com/od/famouschemists

[118] *Architects* design more than buildings. They also design outdoor *spaces*: plazas, parks, pedestrian malls, roadways, transportation centers, and entire. http://www.architecture.about.com/od/urbandesign/u/PublicSpaces.htm

[119] *Obelisks* were prominent in the *architecture* of the ancient Egyptians, who placed them in pairs at the entrance of temples.
http://www.en.wikipedia.org/wiki/Obelisk

[120] A team effort is absolutely essential to any *restoration* project: the owner, the *restoration architect* and each of the artisans that work on it. http://*www.forbes.com* › *ForbesLife* › *Real Estate*

[121] The *ecliptic* plane should be distinguished from the invariable plane of the *solar* system, which is perpendicular to the vector sum of the angular momenta. http://www.en.wikipedia.org/wiki/Ecliptic

122 In *astronomy*, a celestial coordinate system is a coordinate system for mapping, is more often used in *astronomy* and is the complement of the *elevation*. Let (a) be the altitude and (A) the *azimuth* and θ be the zenith (or zenith). http://www.en.wikipedia.org/wiki/Celestial_coordinate_system

123 *nadir* (nā'dər) [Arab.,=opposite], in *astronomy*, the point on the celestial sphere directly opposite the *zenith*, i.e., directly beneath the observer. http://www.www.answers.com/topic/nadir

124 But whilst in *architecture* there was this very great interest in geometry, artists seemed to have lost all interest in the *golden section* and in mathematics. http://www.britton.disted.camosun.bc.ca/goldslide/jbgoldslide.htm

125 *Concrete* is a *composite* building material made from the combination of aggregate, which are used to construct the building *architecture* and supporting. http://www.en.wikipedia.org/wiki/Building_material

126 *Construction* Project *Management* is the overall planning, co-ordination and control of a project from inception to completion aimed at meeting a client's need. http://www.en.wikipedia.org/wiki/Construction_management

127 *Value engineering* (VE) is a systematic method to improve the "value" of goods or products and services by using an examination of function. http://www.en.wikipedia.org/wiki/Value_engineering

128 Much of the current work in cosmology includes understanding how galaxies form in the context of the *Big Bang*, understanding the *physics* of the *Universe* . http://www.en.wikipedia.org/wiki/Big_Bang

129 Lemaître himself also described his theory as "the Cosmic Egg exploding at the moment of the creation"; it became better known as the "Big Bang theory," a term coined by Fred Hoyle. http://en.wikipedia.org/wiki/Georges_Lema%C3%AEtre

130 Based on *Planck's* work, *Einstein* proposed that light also delivers its energy in chunks; light would then consist of little particles, or quanta. http://www.colorado.edu/physics/2000

131 *École des Beaux-Arts* refers to a number of influential art schools in France. The most famous is the École nationale supérieure des Beaux-Arts, http://www.en.wikipedia.org/wiki/École_des_Beaux-Arts

[132] Under an assumption of constant gravity, *Newton's* law of universal *gravitation* simplifies to F = mg, where m is the mass of the body and g is a constant. http://www.en.wikipedia.org/wiki/Gravitation

[133] The combined treatment of classical *mechanics* and *relativity* thus enables the reader to see the connection between Newton's gravitational potential, http://www.worldscibooks.com/physics/6927.html

[134] The life of *Luca Pacioli*: The Father of Accounting. http://www.flynf.tripod.com/pacioli.htm

[135] In the *photoelectric effect*, electrons are emitted from matter (metals and non-metallic solids, liquids or gases) as a consequence of their absorption. http://www.en.wikipedia.org/wiki/Photoelectric_effect

[136] *Mandala*: The *Architecture* of Enlightenment. "Floorplans of the universe," that is exactly what *mandalas* are called in this introduction to an Asia Society. http://www.healing.about.com /.../mandalaorigins /Origins_of_Mandalas_and_Mandala_Drawing.htm

[137] A one-point *perspective drawing* means that the *drawing* has a single vanishing, most often when *drawing architecture* (*architecture* frequently uses lines. http://www.en.wikipedia.org/wiki/Perspective_(graphical)

[138] *Galileo's* sketches of the moon from the *Starry Messenger*. Sidereus Nuncius (usually translated into English as Sidereal Messenger, although *Starry Messenger* http://www.en.wikipedia.org/wiki/Sidereus_Nuncius

[139] In classical electromagnetism, Ampère's circuital law, discovered by André-Marie Ampère in 1826, relates the integrated magnetic field around a closed loop to the electric current passing through the loop. Maxwell derived it again electrodynamically in his 1861 paper *On Physical Lines of Force* and it is now one of the Maxwell equations, which form the basis of classical electromagnetism. http://www.en.wikipedia.org/wiki/Ampère's_circuital_law

[140] The *magnetic field* lines around a long wire which carries an *electric current* form concentric circles around the wire. http://www.hyperphysics.phy-str.gsu.edu/hbase/magnetic/magcur.html

[141] Chemistry question: Why is *diamond hard*? Diamond is the hardest of naturally occurring materials because it is composed of extremely small atoms (carbon) http://www.wiki.answers.com/Q/Why_is_diamond_hard

*Steve Asikin: Wonder of Finance ARCHITECTURE*     213

[142] *durability* ( ˈdurəˈbilədē ) ( engineering ) The quality of equipment, structures, or goods of continuing to be useful after an extended period of.time. http://www.answers.com/topic/durability

[143] The knowledge of modern *geomancy* can be used in the area of nature protection, landscape and *architectural* design, planning of motor ways, in Earth healing. http://www.markopogacnik.com/geomancy.html

[144] *Postmodern architecture* evolved from the modernist movement, yet contradicts many of the modernist ideas. Combining new ideas with traditional forms,
http://www.architecture.about.com/.../Modern-
Architecture/Postmodernism.htm

[145] *Pivot* doors can add keen sense of *architectural* drama and beauty to the most simple spaces and and they work in a variety of homes. http://www.designwonderland.net/blog/?cat=448

[146] Originally, a *landmark* literally meant a geographic feature used by explorers and others to find their way back or through an area. http://www.en.wikipedia.org/wiki/Landmark

[147] There are many common factors that art and *architecture* share, one of which is the *focal point*. Every house or building has its own *focal point*. http://www.lifestyle.iloveindia.com/.../finding-the-focal-point-of-a-room-9485.html

[148] *Rhythm* in *architecture* is the repetitive use of a group of visual elements, at least three times, to establish a recognizable "pattern." http://www.academics.triton.edu/faculty/.../rhythmshoppingcenter.htm

[149] The Greek sun could be seen as one of the governing features in our perception of the *architecture* there. The deep shadows it creates *contrast* with the pale
http://www.greece.org/parthenon/marbles/taylor02.htm

[150] *Architectural composition*; an attempt to order and phrase ideas which hitherto have been only felt by the instinctive taste of designers - Robinson, http://www.archive.org/search.php?...subject%3A%22Architecture%20--
%20Composition%2C%20proportion%2C%20etc%22

[151] *Statics* is the branch of *mechanics* concerned with the analysis of loads (*force*, torque/moment) on physical systems in *static* equilibrium.http://www.en.wikipedia.org/wiki/Statics

[152] *Maxwell's* equations are a set of four partial differential equations that describe how the electric and *magnetic fields* relate to their sources, http://www.en.wikipedia.org/wiki/Maxwell's_equations

[153] An *architect's scale* is a specialized ruler. It is used in making or measuring from reduced *scale* drawings, such as blueprints and floor plans. http://www.en.wikipedia.org/wiki/Architect's_scale

[154] *architectural accentuation* of both global and local field properties. It may well be possible to implement this design for the Kartal. http://www3.interscience.wiley.com/journal/122468114/articletext?DOI=10...

[155] From the very beginning *Architecture* and *proportion* have been closely intertwined. For Auguste Rodin, *proportion* was the synthesis of all the arts. http://www.proportions.de/

[156] The waste water and urine from stables, etc. may be conducted away by gutters sunk in the floor. These gutters are usually made of cast iron. http://www.chestofbooks.com/architecture/Building.../Stable-Drainage.html

[157] The application of engineering to the control of environmental conditions related to public health, such as water supply, sewage, and industrial waste.

http://www.answers.com/topic/sanitary-engineering

[158] The *path* will most likely be wide enough for at least two people to walk abreast. The formal *garden path* is part of the *architecture* of the *garden*. http://www.howtodothings.com/.../how-to-design-a-garden-path

[159] Sited delimited by the *access* road on the East, North and Northwest sides, composition of cubic blocks and *oblique* walls following different angles. http://www.architeria.com/tag/oblique-walls

[160] Biological, FEng Shui and sacred geometry based *architecture*. Dedicated to creating dwellings for the support and advancement of it's occupants. http://www.holisticarchitecture.com/

[161] DuPont analysis (also known as the DuPont identity, DuPont equation, DuPont Model or the DuPont method) is an expression which breaks ROE (Return On Equity) into three parts. The name comes from the DuPont Corporation that started using this formula in the 1920s. http://en.wikipedia.org/wiki/DuPont_analysis

[162] *Galileo* discovered that freely falling bodies, heavy or light, have the same, constant acceleration and that this acceleration is due to *gravity*. www.talktalk.co.uk/reference/encyclopaedia/.../m0003841.html

[163] When he saw the apple fall, *Newton* began to think about a specific kind of motion—*gravity*. *Newton* understood that *gravity* was the force of attraction. http://www.inventors.about.com/library/inventors/blnewton.htm

[164] *Einstein* himself expressed this view on occasions. On this view, we may reasonably hope for a *theory of everything* which self-consistently incorporates all http://www.en.wikipedia.org/wiki/Theory_of_everything

[165] *Architecture* is now emerging that is an *artistic*, somewhat chaotic blending envisioned and brought to reality by several outstanding http://www.fineartregistry.com/.../chaos-merges-with-artistic-architecture-beautifully/ -

[166] With the emerging knowledge in scientific fields and the rise of new materials and *technology*, *architecture* and engineering began to separate. http://www.en.wikipedia.org/wiki/Architecture

[167] In Europe megalithic monuments thousands of years old (*shamanic* cultural *architecture* with practical and spiritual purposes) were defaced, dismantled. http://www.tattooheaven.com/shaman.html

[168] The Geospatial Portal *Reference Architecture* describes a framework within which an organized *collection* of open standard specifications can be implemented. http://www.portal.opengeospatial.org/files/?artifact_id=6669

[169] Qin *Dynasty Great Wall* can be divided into three sections: western, middle and eastern, which took about nine years to finish this grand project. http://www.travelchinaguide.com/china_great_wall/history/qin/

[170] *Architectural rendering,* or *architectural* illustration, is the art of creating two-dimensional images or animations showing the attributes of a proposed. http://www.en.wikipedia.org/wiki/Architectural_rendering

[171] However, with the advent of smart clients, the choice of *presentation* layer *architecture* is no longer straightforward. Rich clients have evolved into smart. http://www.msdn.microsoft.com/en-us/library/aa480039.aspx

[172] Motivation & Proposed *Architecture.* The *architecture* proposed aims at an efficient management and *distribution* of *resources* between the different nodes. http://www.springerlink.com/index/9q2dgpj6f7cxnflj.pdf

[173] As a builder, *Imhotep* is the first master *architects* who we know by name. He is not only credited as the first *pyramid architect,* who built Djoser's Step. http://www.touregypt.net/featurestories/imhotep.htm

[174] As with any business *capability,* the establishment of an enterprise *architecture capability* can be supported. http://www.opengroup.org/architecture/togaf9-doc/.../chap46.html

[175] Contract Magazine showcases groundbreaking *architecture* and design projects. By incorporating quality products and elements into your *architectural* design, http://www.contractdesign.com/contract/products/architectural.../index.jsp

[176] Today, *anthropometry* plays an important role in industrial design, clothing design, ergonomics and *architecture* where statistical data. http://en.wikipedia.org/wiki/Anthropometry

[177] Changdeokgung, also known as Changdeokgung Palace or *Changdeok* Palace, is set within a large park in Jongno-gu, Seoul, South *Korea.* http://www.en.wikipedia.org/wiki/Changdeokgung

[178] The *Joseon* dynasty ruled the *Korea* Peninsula from 1392 until the Japanese occupation of *Korea* in 1910. *Joseon* rulers were able to fend off a late 16th. http://www.asianhistory.about.com/od/southkorea/p/JoseonDynasty.htm

[179] Chungju multipurpose *dam* which is the largest water project in *Korea* was constructed in the South *Han* river that meanders through the central region. http://www.kncold.or.kr/english/dam/dam2.html

[180] *Panmunjom*, located in Gyeonggi Province, is a village on the de facto border between North and South *Korea*, where the 1953 armistice that halted the *Korean*. http://www.en.wikipedia.org/wiki/Panmunjom

[181] Students Worldwide Learn *Korean* Culture at *Yonsei* · Students from different races and nationalities came together at *Yonsei*, http://www.yonsei.ac.kr/eng/

[182] *Gyeongbokgung*, also known as *Gyeongbokgung* Palace or Gyeongbok Palace, is a royal palace located in northern Seoul, South *Korea*. First constructed in 1394. http://www.en.wikipedia.org/wiki/Gyeongbokgung

[183] An *egg* of *Columbus* or Columbi *egg* refers to a brilliant idea or discovery that seems simple or easy after the fact. The expression refers to a popular story. http://www.en.wikipedia.org/wiki/Egg_of_Columbus

[184] *Busan* was the host city of the 2002 Asian Games and APEC 2005 *Korea*. It was also one of the host cities for the 2002 FIFA World Cup, and is a center. http://www.en.wikipedia.org/wiki/Busan

[185] *Incheon* (*Korean* pronunciation: [in.tɕʰʌn]), officially the *Incheon* Metropolitan City, is South *Korea*'s third largest metropolis, after Seoul and Busan. http://www.en.wikipedia.org/wiki/Incheon

[186] *Gwangju* (officially known as *Gwangju* Metropolitan City; *Korean* pronunciation: [kwaŋdzu]) is the sixth largest city in South *Korea*. http://www.en.wikipedia.org/wiki/Gwangju

[187] Koguryo was an ancient *Korean* empire whose brilliant history flourished on a vast expanse of land in East Asia. *Goguryeo* thrived for 705 years from 37 B.C., http:// www.mygoguryeo.net/history.htm

[188] *Baekjae*. Baekje or Paekche, 18 BCE – 660 CE was a kingdom located in southwest *Korea*. It was one of the Three Kingdoms of *Korea*, http://www.servinghistory.com/topics/Baekjae

[189] *Silla* (57 BC – 935 AD) (*Korean* pronunciation: [ɕil a]) was one of the Three Kingdoms of *Korea*, and one of the longest sustained dynasties in Asian history. http://www.en.wikipedia.org/wiki/Silla

[190] Taking clues from aspects of *mainstream*/commercial developments that are not traces of high *architecture* but rather enforced deviations is a useful. http://www.patrikschumacher.com/Texts/hunchsurveyresponse.htm

[191] The *Mercedes* factory tour in *Stuttgart* (singelfinden) is also good, *Plants* bought in Aalsmeer this morning will be in flower shops around the world. http://www.ricksteves.com/graffiti/archives/factorytours.htm

[192] *DaimlerChrysler* was founded in 1998 when Mercedes-Benz manufacturer Daimler-Benz (1926–1998) of Stuttgart, Germany merged with the US-based Chrysler. http://www.en.wikipedia.org/wiki/Daimler_AG

[193] The *Kunstmuseum Stuttgart* is a recently opened (March 2005) art museum in Stuttgart, Germany. The cubic museum building with 5000 m² of display space. http://www.en.wikipedia.org/wiki/Kunstmuseum_Stuttgart

[194] Artist *Nikolaus Koliusis* created a light installation for a tunnel. The lighting imparts a sense of identity to this non-place and facilitates (underground). http://www.mimoa.eu/projects/.../Light%20Installation%2050KM.H

[195] Open source travel guide to *Stuttgart*, featuring up-to-date information on ... Public transportation is provided by the Stadtbahn (*U-bahn*) and S-Bahn. http://www.wikitravel.org/en/Stuttgart

[196] There are over 400 "*Stäffele*" or flights of steps in *Stuttgart*. Anyone wishing to climb them all will have to tackle a total of 20 kilometres of steps. http://www.stuttgart.de/item/show/339480

[197] *Copernicus* therefore incorporated some "Ptolemaic" modifications, by shifting the centers of his circular *orbits* some distance off the Sun, http://www.phy6.org/stargaze/Ssolsys.htm

[198] *Schocken Department Stores* (Kaufhaus Schocken) was a chain of department stores in Germany before the Second World War. Schocken Shopping Centre in Chemnitz. http://www.en.wikipedia.org/wiki/Schocken_Department_Stores

[199] There are some real trophies in the collection: the *Gro?stadt triptych* that was the inspiration for the opening and closing scenes of Cabaret, http://www.travelintelligence.com/.../stuttgart-art-and-architecture

[200] *Guggenheim* Museum constitutes the very core of the institution., the Staatsgalerie *Stuttgart* and the Kunsthalle Bielefeld organized a major Kosuth http://www.guggenheim.org/new-york/...full/bio/?

[201] The shopping and business centre '*Königsbau Passagen*' ('Königsbau' arcades) is part of the extensive urban reorganization of Stuttgart's city centre. http://www.hascherjehle.de/.../koenigsbau-passage-with-stilwerk-stuttgart.html

[202] As Pedestrian Take a walk through the pedestrian subway »Klett-Passage« in direction *Kriegsbergstrasse* / Friedrichstrasse / Heilbronner Strasse. http://www.kronenpat.de/en/kontakt.php

[203] *Socrates* was, above all things, a reformer. He was alarmed at the condition of affairs in Athens, a condition which he was, perhaps, right in ascribing. http://www.en.wikipedia.org/wiki/Socrates; http://*www.newadvent.org;*

[204] The *Bavarian architecture* shows historical evidence of more than 1200 years of history. It ranges from the 8th century ring crypt of St. Emmeran. http://www.guide-to-bavaria.com/en/Bavaria-Culture.html

[205] Built for Louis II of *Bavaria*. Provides a wealth of fairytale storybook images, though considered .as GreatBuildings. http://www.greatbuildings.com/buildings/Neuschwanstein_Castle.html

[206] In 1832 Ludwig's father King Maximilian II of *Bavaria* bought its ruins to replace them by the comfortable neo-Gothic palace known as *Hohenschwangau Castle*. http://www.en.wikipedia.org/wiki/Neuschwanstein_Castle

[207] But according to the Bayerische Biergartenverordnung (*Bavarian* beer garden). The term "beer garden" (*Biergarten*) has become a generic term for open-air. http://www.en.wikipedia.org/wiki/Beer_garden

[208] The *Bavarian Alpine* Foreland (bayerische Alpenvorland) refers to the region of plateau and rolling foothills south of the Danube and north of the Bavarian.http://www.en.wikipedia.org/wiki/Bavarian_Alpine_Foreland

[209] The Bayerisches National *Museum* is toward the Isar River, just east of yet another *Munich* art *museum*, the Haus der Kunst. The city tourist office calls.

http://www.europeforvisitors.com/munich/guide/munich-museums.htm;
http://www.deutsches-museum.de/

210 Any *public place* that is peaceful and has a gravel ground is good enough for boule! The Park of the Residenz—a former castle—is one such example in *Munich*. http://www.ideoeyesopen.com/assignments/story/aging_munich/

211 Nightlife on *Maximiliansplatz, Munich*. Get real opinions, photos, and recommendations for businesses like Jimmy's and Jimmy's. http://www.qype.co.uk/de212/categories/2-nightlife/.../maximiliansplatz

212 Situated at the heart of the Olympiapark München in northern *Munich*, the Olympiastadion was the main venue for the 1972 Summer Olympics. http://www.mimoa.eu/.../Munich/Olympic%20Stadium%20Munich

213 *Isar River* at its source in the Karwendelgebirge (mountains), *Bavaria*, Germany [ *river, Bavaria* Land (state), southern Germany. Rising at an elevation. http://www.britannica.com/EBchecked/topic/295180/Isar-River

214 *Munich Olympic* Stadium With Frei Otto's Roof - Thomas Taylor ... *Olympics*, the tensile glass *tent*-like roof was a lightweight *structure*. http://www.suite101.com/content/the-best-olympic-stadium-architecture-a185283

215 München *Hauptbahnhof* (translated from German as *Munich* Central Station, short form: München Hbf) is the *Hauptbahnhof* (main railway station) of *Munich*. http://www.en.wikipedia.org/wiki/München_Hauptbahnhof

216 Visitors to *Nuremberg* can learn about the Nazi Germany at the new documentation center located at Hitler's convention site, but also discover the medieval. http://www.dw-world.de/dw/article/0,,2332911,00.html

217 Naval *architecture* is an engineering discipline dealing with the design, construction and repair of marine vehicles. Naval *architecture* involves basic and advance. http://www.en.wikipedia.org/wiki/Naval_architecture

218 Like its stable mate, *Mitsubishi's Zero* Fighter the Hamaki soldiered on long after it. Both *aircraft* had unprecedented range but they were also extremely. For the remainder of the *war*, the BETTY assembly line continued

*Steve Asikin: Wonder of Finance ARCHITECTURE*

to run. Admiral Isoroku Yamamoto, *architect* of the Pearl Harbor attack.
www.diggerhistory.info/pages-air-support/ww2.../betty.htm
The present invention relates to an improved *architecture* for an *aircraft*. The *aircraft* has a first engine, a first gearbox associated.
http://www.freepatentsonline.com/6704625.html

[219] An early nuclear power plant that used *atomic* energy to generate electricity, both of which affected the nuclear power *industry* for decades thereafter. Group dedicated to preserving *Atomic* Age culture and *architecture*.
http://www.en.wikipedia.org/wiki/Atomic_Age

[220] To identify and describe different solutions regarding a new *power system architecture* (both the logical and the physical architecture).
http://www.energynautics.com/.../new_power_system_architecture/

[221] *Architecture* coating, spray paint, carb cleaner and more.
http://www.sanvo.en.alibaba.com/

[222] *MEIJI ARCHITECTURE* AND THE EFFECT OF CROSS-CULTURAL. EXCHANGE WITH THE WEST. By Christine Manzano Visita. "Here, now, comes the greatest revolutionary epoch.
http://www.digitalcommons.calpoly.edu/cgi/viewcontent.cgi?article=1007&context

[223] Historians of Meiji and *Taisho architecture* have frequently concentrated on large-scale institutional works of the type that drew the explicit sponsorship
http://www.digitalcommons.calpoly.edu/cgi/viewcontent.cgi?article=1031

[224] Located in the residential *Showa*-cho area of the city, the project aims to create As with any piece of design, be that *architecture*,
http://www.dezeen.com/2010/.../a-house-in-showa-cho-by-shintaro-fujiwara/

[225] tween keiretsu and nonkeiretsu firms. In particular the *keiretsu architecture* may lead to the threat of takeover being a less efficient instrument.
http://www3.interscience.wiley.com/journal/122685597/articletext?DOI=10

[226] *Polymer architecture*. A polymer was defined in the previous section as a macromolecule made up of many segments connected together.
http://www.gelfand.web.cmu.edu/scimodules/2._Polymer_architecture.html

227 The Imperial Japanese Navy was sometimes called Nihon *Kaigun* translated to Propaganda, Culture & *Architecture*, Music of the Reich . http://www.forum.axishistory.com/viewtopic.php?t=473

228 Like the *sogo shosha*, Jar- dine Matheson's *architecture* was based on dense interfirm relationships that contributed to the competitive advantage of the firm. http://www.books.google.co.id/books?isbn=0275980359

229 A famous *Japanese* rock garden is at *Ryōan-ji* in northwest Kyoto, *Japan*. The garden is 30 meters, example of *Japanese* Buddhist *architecture*. Architectonic elements. http://www.en.wikipedia.org/wiki/Japanese_rock_garden

230 *Japanese* national treasures at *Todai-ji*. The *architectural* master-works are *Japanese* Buddhist art, and *Japanese* Buddhist temple *architecture*, http://www.en.wikipedia.org/wiki/Tōdai-ji

231 The perfectly proportioned *architecture* of the main structure and adjoining *Shorinji* Kempo, A mix of college and grad students, *Shorinji* Kempo alumni, http://www.jasgp.org/component/option...0/.../search,*/

232 The *Katsura* district of Kyoto has long been favored for villas, and in the Heian period, *Katsura*: Tradition and Creation in *Japanese Architecture,* http://www.en.wikipedia.org/wiki/Katsura_Imperial_Villa

233 Architecture during the *Nara* period (710-794) was influenced by the Tang style still attempting to keep the aspect of traditional *Japanese architecture*. http:// www.asianinfo.org/asianinfo/japan/pro-architecture.htm

234 A wonder of modern *architecture*, standing at 173 metres high, the Umeda Sky Building in the city of *Osaka*, *Japan* features a "floating garden" on the 39th". http://www.travel-destination-pictures.com/umeda-sky-building-japan-architecture-1427-pictures.htm

235 The Ohiroma of Nijo Castle (17th century) in *Kyoto* is one of the classic *Architecture* and Authority in *Japan*. Nissan Institute/Routledge Japanese. http://www.en.wikipedia.org/wiki/Japanese_architecture

236 That is certainly not to say that *Tokyo* is without its *architectural* gems, far from it, this is *Japan* after all. A convenient and spectacular example. http://www.citynoise.org/article/2675

[237] *Yokohama* Now *Japan's* second largest city, a bustling metropolis with a thriving port and a stunning waterfront,
http://www.emporis.com/application/?nav=city&lng=3&id=yokohama-japan

[238] Meiji *architecture, Nagasaki*. Some of the finest foreign-designed house in *Japan* are situated in Glover Garden, *Nagasaki*. They overlook the site.
http://www.pbase.com/rkphoto/nagameiji

[239] *Sapporo* Art Walk is an art book that focuses on the relationship between art and history of *Sapporo*, not only introducing *architecture* and public art
http://www.shift.jp.org/en/archives/2010/05/sapporo_art_walk.html

[240] *Kobe's* main attraction for the *Japanese* is its concentration of Western-style *houses*, some dating back to the days when *Kobe* was opened for foreign trade. http://www.wiki.worldflicks.org/kobe.html